"The Object Lessons series ___ to magic: the books take o ___ and animate them with a r ___ political struggle, science, ___ Filled with fascinating detai__ ___ conveyed in sharp, accessible prose, the books make the everyday world come to life. Be warned: once you've read a few of these, you'll start walking around your house, picking up random objects, and musing aloud: 'I wonder what the story is behind this thing?'"

Steven Johnson, author of *Where Good Ideas Come From* and *How We Got to Now*

"Object Lessons describes themselves as 'short, beautiful books,' and to that, I'll say, amen.... If you read enough Object Lessons books, you'll fill your head with plenty of trivia to amaze and annoy your friends and loved ones—caution recommended on pontificating on the objects surrounding you. More importantly, though ... they inspire us to take a second look at parts of the everyday that we've taken for granted. These are not so much lessons about the objects themselves, but opportunities for self-reflection and storytelling. They remind us that we are surrounded by a wondrous world, as long as we care to look."

John Warner, *The Chicago Tribune*

OBJECTLESSONS

A book series about the hidden lives of ordinary things.

Series Editors:

Ian Bogost and Christopher Schaberg

In association with

BOOKS IN THE SERIES

Wine

MEG BERNHARD

BLOOMSBURY ACADEMIC
NEW YORK • LONDON • OXFORD • NEW DELHI • SYDNEY

BLOOMSBURY ACADEMIC
Bloomsbury Publishing Inc
1385 Broadway, New York, NY 10018, USA
50 Bedford Square, London, WC1B 3DP, UK
29 Earlsfort Terrace, Dublin 2, Ireland

BLOOMSBURY, BLOOMSBURY ACADEMIC and the Diana logo are
trademarks of Bloomsbury Publishing Plc

First published in the United States of America 2023

Library of Congress Cataloging-in-Publication Data

Names: Bernhard, Meg, author.
Title: Wine / Meg Bernhard.
Description: New York : Bloomsbury Academic, 2023. | Series: Object lessons | Includes bibliographical references and index. | Summary: "Structured around the seasons, Wine draws from memoir, journalism, literature, and science to explores humans' deep connection to wine and the nexus of wine and power - from inequalities in the winemaking industry to the forces that determine what and how we drink"– Provided by publisher.
Identifiers: LCCN 2022052329 (print) | LCCN 2022052330 (ebook) | ISBN 9781501383618 (paperback) | ISBN 9781501383625 (ebook) | ISBN 9781501383632 (pdf) | ISBN 9781501383649 (ebook other)
Subjects: LCSH: Wine and wine making–Social aspects. | Wine industry. | Bernhard, Meg.
Classification: LCC TP548 . B373 2023 (print) | LCC TP548 (ebook) | DDC 641.2/2–dc23/eng/20221221
LC record available at https://lccn.loc.gov/2022052329
LC ebook record available at https://lccn.loc.gov/2022052330

ISBN: PB: 978-1-5013-8361-8
         ePDF: 978-1-5013-8363-2
         eBook: 978-1-5013-8362-5

Series: Object Lessons

Typeset by Deanta Global Publishing Services, Chennai, India
Printed and bound in the United States of America

To find out more about our authors and books visit www.bloomsbury.com and sign up for our newsletters.

CONTENTS

PREFACE

" This wine," the historian told me, a glass raised to his nose, "smells like yellow flowers that bloomed in my village when I was a child."

I was having lunch with Joan Gómez Pallarès, a classicist and a wine columnist for Spain's biggest newspaper, at a cavernous bar near the port of Tarragona, a city in the country's northeast. I'd hoped he, a critic renowned for his precise writing, could teach me to be more attentive when I tasted wine. New to both the country and the drink, I struggled to find words to describe the world around me—including what was in my glass. When I sniffed the honey colored liquid Pallarès had ordered for us, my mind went blank. I could detect something, but I didn't have the language to articulate what I was smelling.

Springtime was rapidly approaching. Wildflowers carpeted the hillsides. Meadows were lush green after winter rain. I'd been living on a vineyard in central Spain, and now, Pallarès and I discussed the next vineyard where I would move, a patchwork of vines and scrubland eighty miles north of Barcelona. A child of the suburbs, I was unaccustomed to agricultural work, but Pallarès assured me that the labor would be well worth it: the vineyard was a sensory wonderland, a place where I could learn to smell and speak.

I grew up fifty miles northeast of San Diego, near the desert. Temecula, my hometown, is a dry place that, on average, receives about fourteen inches of rain a year, and also an increasingly hot one, with summer temperatures regularly exceeding 100 degrees Fahrenheit. The heat was a basic fact of life when I was a child. The hottest months were, roughly, April to November. Summer afternoons were meant for lying on cold tile, under the air-conditioning vent. At night, my mother would turn on portable fans and give me a wet washcloth, and we slept on top of our sheets, sweating. October was still hot, the Santa Ana winds kicking up dust and smoke from distant wildfires. Finally, in December, temperatures were low enough to hike comfortably in the afternoon. We had snowfall just once, when I was nine. When I looked out the window that morning, I saw bits of white flutter in the air like confetti, then melt on the driveway.

My home seemed a place estranged from the natural world. We were so close to rich and varied landscapes—the Anza-Borrego Desert, the Mojave, the kelp forests off the San Diego coast—and yet I spent most of my time in man-made spaces: soccer fields, swimming pools, malls and movie theaters. My father, a commuter, spent hours each day stuck in Orange County traffic. While my mother worked locally, she still spent most of her waking hours at the office, in front of a computer screen. And though we lived in the country's bread basket—I was born in Fallbrook, California, self-proclaimed Avocado Capital of the World—we purchased pre-packaged, all-season meals from garish supermarkets. We lived in what the British anthropologist E.E. Evans-Pritchard calls "structural time," its rhythms derived from the social world.[1] We had no sense of "ecological time," the cadence of the natural environment. Mostly, I experienced the natural world as lack—of water, of trees, of any color other than brown.

My perspective changed when I moved to Spain. For two years, I lived in the country, first for several months on a vineyard in Castilla-La Mancha, then for several more on a vineyard in L'Albera. The rest of the time I spent traveling, or living in Barcelona, retuning to vineyards to help with seasonal tasks. When the coronavirus pandemic hit, I moved back to California.

Working with vines that first year in Spain, I began to live in both structural and ecological time. My life revolved around a vineyard's rhythms. I moved when the seasons changed. Late fall, when I arrived in central Spain, was time for cellar work: bottling, packing, and shipping the wine. In February, we pruned the vines with electric clippers. Springtime, when I lived at the foot of the Pyrenees Mountains, was for removing excess leaves from the vine; the sticky summer months were for watering and upkeep. Long-awaited was *vendimia*—the harvest.

WINTER

Castilla-La Mancha

Stick Season

What to call the time of transition between fall and winter? Stick season, a friend in Vermont once told me—the time when leaves have fallen and trees are naked, but before the snow.

It was stick season when I arrived, one crisp November morning several years ago, to work on a small family vineyard in Castilla-La Mancha, a region in central Spain. I'd wanted to live in Spain for years, after I first visited when I was eighteen while writing for a travel guide. Now twenty-one, I was amazed to learn that my university offered open-ended travel grants centered around a project of the recipient's design. Searching for a way to get to Spain, I'd proposed a project that involved working on vineyards, even though I knew nothing about wine. I had a vague feeling why vineyard work might be good for my mind and body, but that wouldn't become clear until later.

The winemaker Carmen López Delgado, 4'11 and wrapped in a thick camel coat, waited for me on a train platform in the town of Torrijos, population 14,000. Her hair was curled and brown with golden streaks, and her lips were deep burgundy. She looked regal. She welcomed me with a long hug, as though we had known each other for years. The month before, I sent her an email asking if I could volunteer on her vineyard; she responded promptly with an invitation to live in her home. I was to help with the winter cellar work: bottling and packaging wines, translating information for their website.

Carmen led me out of the train station and into the bustling town center. A line of stalled cars curved around the block, and a half dozen department stores advertised discounted purses. Women carrying bulky shopping bags buzzed into apartment buildings, and elderly men and women sat in a plaza, reading newspapers, sipping coffee, and chatting. A man grilled chestnuts and offered them wrapped in newsprint—two euros for six.

We stopped at the butcher. Inside, a woman wearing a hairnet was chopping the legs off a skinned rabbit. Behind her hung a muscular leg of ham, frail ankle and hoof still attached. Carmen bent to examine the meats and cheeses displayed in the glass case under the counter and pointed to a mound of yellow cheese. "This is typical here," she told me, handing the butcher a few euros for the cheese. "It's queso manchego, curado."

We next walked to a nearby bakery. The store was warm, heat emanating from ovens in the back room. Carmen held each loaf of bread up to her nose, pressing her thumbs into the soft middle that pushed through hard outer crust. She bought two loaves, as well as a bag of muffins called magdalenas, an assortment of marzipan—also typical of the region, she said—and flaky cookies shaped like two outspread palms, called palmeras.

After another few blocks, we arrived at her flat. The apartment was long, with a balcony overlooking the main square and a bright kitchen stocked with an assortment of teas and milk bottles containing grape juice she'd pasteurized a few months earlier. A small wine refrigerator in the living room held colorfully labeled bottles. These were wines she'd acquired at fairs around Europe, after bartering her own in exchange. I'd try many of them, she promised.

Friday Nights

On my second evening in Castilla-La Mancha, Carmen's husband Luis drove us to an unassuming bar just off the highway. In the fading light, I could see miles of vineyards, their vines gnarled and naked. We sat by a candy dispenser in the back of the bar and a few of Carmen's childhood friends arrived, all of them three decades older than me. The bartender brought us small glasses of beer, called cañas, and

Luis uncorked a bottle of his and Carmen's wine, red made from Graciano grapes. Carmen pulled a head of fermented garlic out of her purse. The skin was brown and soft, left to age in humid heat. Carmen had gotten the bulb from a winemaker friend who fermented garlic as a side project. "It's a natural antibiotic," she told us. "Taste it, you'll be surprised." She passed us each a piece. I turned mine between my fingers and peeled open the skin, and the garlic underneath was black, thick and sticky as molasses, staining my thumb. On my tongue, the mass dissolved into a tangy syrup, and its fleeting sweetness faded.

Friday nights at the bar became my classroom. Carmen would uncork three or four bottles, sometimes her own wine—strong, liquory Gracianos, and Tempranillos meant for the wintertime—or wine from her friends in Catalonia and Córdoba and Alsace, places that seemed a world away. The wine helped me imagine these places. The French word *terroir*, Carmen told me, meant that the wine should reveal something essential about where it came from. A briny wine made from the grape Malvasia de Sitges could take me to a vineyard by the Mediterranean. An acidic wine made from Albariño grapes could take me to the lush, steep canyons of Galicia.

We ate, we always ate: cured meats and cheese, or patatas bravas, or tortillas españolas. Carmen would pass around glasses she had brought from home (the owner of the bar was a childhood friend who permitted our weekly ritual) and led us through a tasting. She would tell us to hold the glass up to the light to examine the wine's color—*Look how purple this is, she said, like a queen's robes.* Then, we would bring our nose to the glass and offer words to describe what we smelled: flowers, berries, cedar, orange peel. "Smell is the human sense most strongly associated with memory," Carmen told me. What we smelled in wine was deeply personal. She quizzed me on what I smelled and I would search for the few familiar aromas I had tucked away in my memory.

"This," Carmen said one night as she put her nose to a glass of her own Graciano aged for a few months in oak barrels, "smells like chicken blood, just like when my mother used to cut off hens' heads and drain their blood into a bucket." We laughed, shook our heads. We did not smell the blood.

The last step was to drink. Carmen closed her eyes when she did this, and when she liked a wine she smiled with her whole face. "This one makes me happy," she would say. Another would surprise her, tickle her. From her I learned wines should make you feel something—nostalgia or homesickness or delight or passion. Wines that provoked an emotional response made the best sort of conversation. The worst review a wine could receive was silence at the table afterward.

First Drink

I'd had my first taste of wine just a few years earlier, when I was eighteen. It was late winter, and I was sitting on frozen ground with my college roommate, the two of us bundled in heavy coats. We were in Central Park, near her mother's apartment. Using a fake ID, my roommate had bought what I later learned was Prosecco from a corner store, along with plastic cups. She poured stealthily, instructing me to hide my cup if a cop walked by.

Though the circumstances were not lavish, drinking cheap wine in New York felt immeasurably luxurious. At the time, I earned a hundred dollars a week at the student newspaper. I made another couple hundred a week working at a laundry service, where I collected bags of dirty clothes from outside student dorm rooms and loaded them into a cart to deliver to the laundromat.

The wine's color was dim. Fizz sparked and then settled in my mouth. My head felt light, and my bare hands were raw from the cold. I didn't have any words to describe the taste of the wine, hadn't yet learned there was an entire vocabulary for the drink. Instead, I described to my friend how I felt drinking alcohol for the first time—giddy.

After that first taste, I drank whatever alcohol was handed to me at parties. Most of the wine I drank in college was cheap, boxes and liter bottles procured semi-legally for the purpose of binge-drinking. Every once in a while, wine transcended sweaty dorm room parties and entered the realm of the elite, during meet and greets with artists and bankers and academics. The people at these events treated wine as an object of study. They seemed to have a secret lexicon, using corporeal words like *body* and *legs* or words

I'd never heard at all, like *Sauv Blanc* and *Pinot Gris*. Back then, when I drank, I was not so discerning. I drank to lose language, not to learn it.

After my twenty-first birthday, I started ordering wine in restaurants. Sommeliers used words I did not recognize and taste descriptions I could not detect in the wine's flavor. Observing other diners, I noticed that waiters chose one person for the first pour—the person, it seemed, who projected a greater degree of authority over the meal, and who was therefore granted the ability to accept or decline a bottle of wine. That person would smell, sip, pause, and nod. There was, it appeared, a choreography to wine drinking, a push and pull of power.

Speaking Underwater

Languages come to me slowly. Eight years of Spanish in high school and college gave me only the most basic of sentences, primarily questions: How are you? What is your job? Are you going to the beach this summer?

With Carmen, I learned faster out of necessity; she didn't speak English. We'd have breakfast together in her flat, drinking coffee with almond milk and watching the news. She'd talk about her family or dole out observations on relationships. A favorite saying of hers was *Nuestras parejas son espejos,* our partners are mirrors. I would offer a sentence or two, but mostly I listened. Then we'd clean up. Once, while clearing the table, I asked where the napkins went. *El cajón*, she told me, enunciating slowly as she pointed. The drawer. Those were my lessons.

Communicating in Spanish felt like trying to hold a conversation underwater. Some evenings, I sat at the dinner table and struggled to follow what Carmen's family was saying, their words familiar yet just beyond the threshold of comprehension. Other times, however, the conversation was perfectly clear. My progress toward fluency was halting, and I made many mistakes. I understood less when I was tired, more after I'd had coffee. But Carmen was patient. "Look how much you've learned," she'd say.

When we had no work to do, Carmen told me stories of her past. She had been a stay-at-home mom when she became sick with cancer. There are no pictures from this time, when she didn't have hair, a conscious attempt at forgetting.

She says the land saved her. In 2005, while still sick, she bought 13 and a half hectares in her hometown of Santa Olalla from her mother and a neighboring farmer. To start the project—which involved renting equipment and cellar space—she and Luis borrowed money from their parents. Over the following years, the couple contracted an agricultural services company to help plant the vineyard, a small tract of Tempranillo and a larger parcel of Graciano. Within a few years, they were harvesting.

The region, its soil clay and limestone, saw scarce precipitation. Summers were hot and dry; winters were cold. Carmen talked about the land as though it was divine.

Nature, she said, nurtures us, and spending time outdoors returns us to our truest selves. Vineyard work was peaceful, invigorating. It gave her the energy to focus on recovery. I asked when we'd see the vineyard. Soon, she said.

¿Qué Significa?

One of my early tasks was to translate Carmen's technical sheets, which described the vineyards and wines, into English. Sitting in Carmen's living room with the printed-out sheets and a Spanish-to-English dictionary, I imagined the land: 492 meters above sea level, oriented on an east-west axis. Each of these elements, Carmen told me, influence the taste of a wine.

I collected dozens of words while doing this work. *Cepa* was an individual grape vine. *Pie americano* was American rootstock—resistant to phylloxera, the blight that decimated Europe's vineyards in the nineteenth century. *Viña espaldera* was a trellised vine, supported by a wire. *La crianza* was aging, often by barrel. Most beautiful of all was *vendimia*, the word for grape harvest. Other crops had *cosecha* or *recogida* for their harvests, but the grape merited its own term.

Carmen's wine fell under the umbrella of "natural," or, as other people call it, "minimum intervention." More of a philosophy than a stable definition, such wines, which have no regulatory body determining what is and is not "natural," are generally made from grapes grown without pesticides, and have no chemical additions during the winemaking process itself—except, perhaps, a small amount of sulfites to keep the wine stable for overseas shipment. Natural wine comprises a limited share of the global wine market, but, over the past decade, it's gained in popularity within the United States and around the world, from Europe to South America. Translating Carmen's sheets, I encountered other words associated with natural wine: *levadura autóctona, fermentación espontánea, sin filtración ni clarificación*—native yeast, spontaneous fermentation, no filtration or clarification.

Certain words stumped me, requiring a multilevel translation from Spanish to technical English and then to more colloquial English. *Añada*, Google Translate told me, meant "vintage." Like clothing? I assumed it was an error on Google's part, so, using context clues, I translated it to "year." I wasn't too far off—vintage, I later learned, refers to the year when the wine's grapes were harvested. Some days, Carmen and Luis would siphon wine from one tank to the next—a *trasiego*, or, I learned in English, racking, meant to separate the liquid from sediment.

Learning what these technical words meant was an even clumsier process than simply learning Spanish. Reading them on paper, or hearing them spoken, rarely gave me the context necessary to understand their definitions. Some terms—*brut, cuvée, élevage*—were left, untranslated, in French, another language I didn't know. I didn't grow up in a family that drank wine, so I had never heard most of these words until I was surrounded by people who dropped them into conversation. I used the same phrase over and over: *¿Qué significa?* What does that mean?

Castilla-La Mancha

The region in which Torrijos is located, Castilla-La Mancha, produces more wine than anywhere else in Spain.[1] With nearly half a million acres of planted vineyard, it's also considered the world's largest contiguous wine region[2]. Around the world, wine-producing regions are divided up into country-specific categories, each with their own set of laws governing how winemakers are permitted to make their wine. In Spain and Chile, they're called Denominaciones de origen (DOs); in France, **Appellations d'origine contrôlée (AOCs)**; in the United States, American Viticultural Areas (AVAs). France, home to some of the strictest regulations, developed their system of zoning in the early 1900s. In the decades prior, after the blight of North American-born insects known as phylloxera destroyed some forty percent of French grapevines, wine production plummeted, and people began selling low-quality wine masquerading as the country's finest, with grapes sourced from far outside the regions where wine labels claimed they had originated. The AOC system was therefore intended to preserve the notion of terroir, that a wine from a certain place is unique, and to prevent fraud.[3]

Today, winemakers wishing to use, for example, the word "Champagne" on their labels are only permitted to use certain grape varieties and select modes of pruning their vines. They may only harvest and press up to a certain quantity of grapes. The style of the wine, too, is precise: a Champagne must undergo two fermentations, the second of which occurs in the bottle (as opposed to a tank or barrel, where fermentations normally take place), and at least fifteen months up to three years of aging. The grapes must be planted within the Champagne region of France.[4]

Carmen makes her wine under the regulatory label "Vino de la Tierra de Castilla," a category below the Denominación de Origen Castilla-La Mancha. Historically, Castilla-La Mancha has produced bulk wine, which, instead of being bottled, is shipped off in large trucks for bottling or boxing elsewhere. Wine from Castilla-La Mancha has a reputation for being lower quality, drunk for two or three euros a bottle on street corners and plazas. This public drinking ritual, popular among teenagers and similar to my own first experience drinking in Central Park, is known as *botellón*. But the wines Carmen showed me were rich and steeped in regional culture. Everyone I met in Castilla-La Mancha knew someone who worked in wine; most people themselves had worked harvests growing up to earn some extra cash. They knew the land well—its rolling hills, dispersed with vines and olive trees and fields of grain, each crop essential to the region's economy. Castilla-La Mancha's red wines paired well with homemade croquetas—meat-and-potato-filled dumplings—or hearty stews, humble yet delicious meals meant to feed the region's farmworkers.

Paciencia

Carmen's cellar was located about thirteen miles northeast of Torrijos. The space was narrow with high ceilings. Seven steel tanks, each holding ten or fifteen thousand liters of wine, crowded the floor. Thousands of black glass bottles rested in iron crates, stacked one atop the other. A dozen French oak barrels, inscribed in chalk with the words *gratitud*, *amor*, and *paciencia* sat next to the bottles. Each year, Carmen made some 30,000 or 40,000 bottles—a large quantity for a small producer, but nothing compared to the more than 12 million bottles one of the country's largest winemakers, Catalonia-based Bodega Torres, makes annually. Major wineries employ hundreds of people to work at their facilities, but Carmen and Luis generally worked alone, or with the help of their four children. During the grape harvest, they contracted a dozen or so day laborers who they paid 80 euros for eight hours of work, minimum wage in Castilla-La Mancha.

Our work in the cellar felt detached from land and memory. We acted as an assembly line. We bottled and labeled and packaged wine for shipment to small bars and individual customers around Europe. We siphoned wine from one tank to the next.

This work would all make sense during the harvest, Carmen assured me. I would cut the grapes and see them pressed, fruit crushed and steeping in their juices. After a few days off the vine, grapes would begin to ferment: the wild yeasts that dwelled on their skins would convert sugar into alcohol.

One afternoon, Carmen poured me a glass. The wine was made in 2017, from Graciano grapes. I took a sip. My face blushed and my forehead tingled. The wine was heady. Dense. Alcohol near 15 percent. It tasted of *sequía*, Carmen said. Drought. Thirsty vines produce fewer and smaller grapes than normal, and sugar becomes concentrated in those few grapes. Drought makes wine deeper, richer, and more alcoholic.

The year 2017 was the hottest in Spain since 1965.[5] Reservoirs evaporated, rivers ran dry. The cobbled remains of Santa Marta, a village in a lush part of the country, emerged from the man-made lake that had engulfed them for decades. Farmers mourned their ruined crops. Yet the sky gave little.

Wine, Carmen said, tells the story of the land, of the year. It tells of dryness and wetness, storms and serenity. The taste of the year is subtle, present in the sweetness, the bitterness, the acidity of the drink. Such flavors are legible to the people who know to taste for them. By the end of winter, I was beginning to learn.

Recuperation

On my birthday, I finally saw the vineyard. It was a crisp afternoon in early December. Carmen's vines were southwest of Santa Olalla, spreading down a gentle hill. The Sierra de Gredos Mountains rose in the distance.

Vines were strung together on a long wire. Their naked trunks were twisted, branches searching. I ran my hand over the bark in wonder. Just a few months before, those branches had held grape bunches, yet it was hard to imagine the wood was alive.

Do not underestimate the winter, Carmen told me. Winter is the season of recuperation. No longer growing leaves and grapes, the vine's roots would stretch deep into the soil, soaking nutrients and preparing for springtime growth. Carmen instructed me to watch how vines grow: slowly at first, then quickly, a rush of green and gold and burgundy. In the winter, vines appear dead, stripped of their leaves and fruit. In the spring, as wildflowers push through the dirt, green shoots and buds emerge from the wood. In the summer, grapes grow rapidly, canopies of leaves transforming Castilla-La Mancha's brown hillsides. The fall arrives in deep purples and pale yellows, the colors of mature grapes. The beauty of the vineyard is witnessing the cycle of seasons. To witness that simple fact of nature is to take part in the vine's long history of cultivation. Tracing my hands across a gnarled trunk, I felt the pull of time.

Classicists link the life cycle of the grapevine to Dionysian myths. According to these myths, Dionysus, the Greek god of wine, experienced a "double birth." The mortal Semele, Princess of Thebes, was preparing to give birth to Dionysus when her lover Zeus appeared to her in god form, riding his chariot. Mortals could not look upon gods without perishing, so Semele died, incinerated by Zeus's lightning bolt. Zeus saved the fetus, Dionysus, by sewing him into his thigh. Dionysus eventually sprang from his father's body.[6] In another myth of double birth, Titans rip apart Dionysus, a son of Zeus and Persephone, and devour his body—except for the heart. From that heart he was born again.[7]

On Carmen's vineyard, I took a photo of the quiet landscape—the dry earth, the brittle branches. Months later, when the vines would burst with ochre and crimson fruit, I wanted to remember the time and place, the absence of it all, from which life had emerged.

Natural History

It's ancient, the idea that agriculture and climate and place are all bound up in the taste of a wine. The Roman writer Pliny the Elder, in his behemoth thirty-seven book work *Naturalis historia* (*Natural History*), offers an account of what was then known about wine—the vine's cultivation, the different types of wines found around the Mediterranean, the various ways to prepare and store the drink. He was particularly in awe of the vine, writing that there was not "a wood in existence of a more lasting nature than this," nor a "perfume known which in exquisite sweetness can surpass" the aroma of a flowering grapevine. He expanded on his contemporary Columella's notion of terroir, contending, for example, that the "black earth which prevails in Campania is not everywhere found suited to the vine," suggesting, in other words, that different soils in different places won't grow the same quality of grapes.[8]

Each of *Natural History*'s volumes probes some element of nature, at once interrogating and appreciating. Reading Pliny's work, I'm drawn to a small and lyrical selection: the table of contents for Book Two, called "An account of the world and the elements." The list reads like a poem; chapters one through three examine whether the world is finite, as well as the world's "shape; its motion; reason for its name," while further chapters discuss "The elements. God . . . The stars—their distances apart . . . Music from the stars . . . Dimensions of the world . . . sky-yawning . . . Rivers—their reason . . . Retreat of sea, where occurred?"

I hear in his curiosity echoes of my own. After I visited Carmen's vineyard, I began to look at wine differently. Drinking new bottles, I recalled the chalky soil that dusted our boots in Santa Olalla. If that parcel of earth had produced her rich red wines, what was the land like in other parts of the country? And the rest of the world? What wines might these places create?

I imagine Pliny the Elder writing in 70 CE, a time so long ago it's at the limits of my comprehension. I imagine him speculating on the nature of winds, the movement of the stars. Then, like now, so much about the universe was uncertain. The world, Pliny seemed to say, is a place of wonder.

"The dirtiest and heaviest work"

The world, Pliny also said, is a place to be conquered. He was an imperialist, a defender of the Roman Empire. Scholars have argued that *Natural History* presented empire as a civilizing force in the world. When Romans conquered new swaths of land, they brought with them agricultural tools to expand wine production.

Elsewhere in the world, the history of wine selling and growing is deeply intertwined with empire and forced labor. The wine industry in South Africa's cape region, for example, was built by slaves. In 1652, Jan van Riebeeck, a Dutch colonizer and Commander of the Cape Colony, wrote that slaves—the first of whom the Dutch East India Company took from Angola in 1658—should "do the dirtiest and heaviest work in place of the Netherlanders."[9] Spanish Franciscan missionaries introduced wine cultivation to California by way of the mission system, forcing enslaved Native Americans to plant vineyards for sacramental wine.[10]

In *A History of Wine in America*, Thomas Pinney quotes one southerner in the 1850s as saying, "With all the facilities we possess at the South, with our soil, climate, and more particularly our slaves, nothing can prevent ours from becoming the greatest wine country that ever was."[11]

None of this was apparent to me my first months in Spain. I was not yet prepared to ask many questions of vineyards— who worked the land, who financed the land, what sorts of people took fruit from the land and profited from it. I was absorbing beauty before I could see complexity.

Sobremesa

In Spain, wine drinking was often spontaneous and informal. On New Year's Eve, I drank four-dollar red wine mixed with coca cola—known as *kalimotxo*—in the street with Carmen's daughter and her friends, broke twenty-year-olds. I drank Carmen's wine on a crisp night in the mountains as we stood around *luminarias*, bonfires kindled by old furniture, meant to release a house's spirits. Later in the year, I would drink wine in vineyards with farmers during work breaks, and from *porrones*, glass wine pitchers, at *calçotadas*, late winter barbecues featuring grilled, stringy vegetables called *calçots*. Everywhere, I met cellar hands who diluted wine with carbonated water and sipped all day.

With Carmen, to drink was to share. Meals with her family lasted up to seven hours. We ate lunches of shrimp, ox, and cod; dinners of jamón serrano, Manchego cheese, olives, and tomatoes. Sometimes, we ate with her mother, or Luis's parents, or at long tables crowded with relatives. Our conversation topics were wide-ranging: politics, feminism, historical memory, the weather. After some meals, we'd spend another hour or two talking and drinking and picking at food. To keep the conversation going, the host would usually bring out a *rancio*, a viscous, sweet drink made by exposing wine to oxygen, or a reductive wine, made with only limited oxygen contact. They'd also bring out pastries, or chocolate, or hard cheese, and we'd all keep drinking for hours, opening more bottles and sipping small cups of coffee to stay awake.

This time after the official meal is called the *sobremesa*, or "over the table." Though it's a uniquely Spanish word, I would later find the spirit of sobremesa in many places: a picnic in the park; chips and beer in an apartment; breakfast on a balcony in a cold city. Even the simple pleasure of one bottle, a few friends, and a sun-warmed patio seems to embody the easy, communal ethos of the sobremesa. To participate in the sobremesa is to savor.

San Francisco

A few years after meeting Carmen, I went to a bar in San Francisco. There, I spoke with a sommelier. He was

American, with a surfer's accent, but he quickly slipped into an incomprehensible lexicon when he described the wine. He spoke of unfamiliar French domaines and châteaus, of a winemaking style from northeastern Italy. Intrigued, I waited for a pause so I could ask questions, but he carried on, his tone indicating he considered his commentary obvious. With each minute that passed, I felt less intelligent.

"You should try this," the sommelier finally said, thrusting an orange colored wine toward me. I took the glass, overwhelmed but relieved. This seemed like a welcoming gesture; instead of intending to make me feel small, he, like Carmen, wanted to share his knowledge and his language.

Until I lived in Spain, I'd never spent much time talking to sommeliers. They'd always seemed standoffish to me, and I distrusted them. Most I met were men. The public face of the wine industry's many gatekeepers, they often pushed me to blow past my budget, to buy more expensive wines because they assumed to understand my taste better than me.

The San Francisco sommelier, though, reminded me of people I'd met in Spain who would pour me free glasses because they enjoyed the conversation and appreciated my curiosity. I presumed the same of him. When I had finished that glass, he poured me a red wine. He kept talking late into the night, so late that I missed the last train home.

I was wrong, in the end. He charged for all the glasses he'd poured, none of which I'd asked for.

Proustian wine

Wine, Carmen taught me, is best experienced as communion: an exchange between people, something to be shared. But the broader industry approach to selling wine that I experienced in San Francisco—tasting notes littered with vocabulary only accessible to people who have the time and money to learn it—is at odds with Carmen's philosophy and the casual and communal experience of the sobremesa. The language of wine has, like any language, the power to exclude. Friends have told me they find the drink intimidating because of its jargon. They assume those who know how to wield that jargon are more sophisticated. Often, such people are also wealthy.

What, and whether, we drink is often an indicator of class. Some people drink wine in upscale settings, at Michelin-starred restaurants and trendy city bars, their bottles costing hundreds of dollars. With Carmen and other Spanish winemakers, drinking wine was commonplace, a bottle on table alongside bread and olive oil. Even people who didn't make wine tended to have a glass at lunch or dinner. But in the United States, I've found wine is often pricier and more exclusive, making its consumption less habitual.

The most expensive standard, or 750 milliliter, bottle of wine ever sold at an auction fetched $558,000 in New York, in 2018. (In 2021, a non-standard six-liter bottle of wine was auctioned for $1 million in New Orleans.)[12] As with other rare goods, vintage wines are often sold at auction for much higher than the market price. One can also purchase "wine futures," investing in a young wine before it has been bottled, its final quality unknown. The half-million-dollar wine was a seventy-three-year-old red from Burgundy, one of the most exclusive wine-producing regions in France, made by the estate Domaine Romanée Conti, considered one of the world's finest producers. The four-and-a-half acre tract of land where the grapes were grown once belonged to the Catholic Church, and later a Bourbon prince; today, it's owned by two families.[13]Writer Richard Olney once called wine from the estate "velvet, seductive and mystery" and "the most Proustian of great wines."[14] Serena Sutcliffe, head of the auction house's international wine department, deemed this particular bottle a "wine at peace with itself" with "seemingly everlasting power."[15] The buyer, whose identity remained anonymous, was simply referred to as a "collector."

The wine wheel

In the 1980s, in an attempt to make wine more accessible to everyday drinkers but still establish a communal language, University of California, Davis chemist Ann C. Noble created what is known as the "Aroma Wheel," a circle containing dozens of possible aromas to be found in wine.[16] "Novice tasters often complain that they 'cannot smell anything' or can't think of a way to describe the aroma of wine," Noble wrote. "They don't have the words!"

Her prompt, intended to solve one problem of wine language, led to another—the proliferation of a certain type of winespeak. Deriving language from a set of key words stifles the imagination, limiting one's sensorial experience of a wine to a series of finite categories. For example, on the wine-rating website and app Vivino, billed as a "marketplace empowering people everywhere to enjoy wine to the fullest," I read the following reviews:

> "Candied cherries with just a hint of blueberry with just a hint of sleet in the finish."

> "Lemon, lime, gin-like spices, bubblegum, lemon grass, ginger, lemon myrtle, very gentle palate, shrewd acidity, medium weight, dry."

> "An expressive bouquet with powerful aromas of blueberries, black cherries, plums and sweet spices. Very full bodied wine with velvety tannins and round on the palate, it has very concentrated flavours of ripe forest fruits and integrated oak."

These notes sounded like others that I was beginning to hear at restaurants or tastings, full of words used so widely and frequently they became meaningless.

Meanwhile, other guides emerged alongside the Wine Wheel's attempt to make a science out of tasting. In its Systematic Approach to Tasting, the Wine and Spirit Education

Trust (WSET), a nonprofit based in the United Kingdom, offers a protocol and a set of terms for how drinkers should taste wine, starting with an examination of the wine's appearance and ending with its flavors.[17]

According to the WSET, a drinker can experience the smells and tastes of a wine in three registers. Under the primary aroma/flavor category, there are subcategories—floral, fruit, herbaceous, herbal, and spice—all of which arise from the grape and alcoholic fermentation. There are many types of fruity wines that can evoke anything from banana to, rather obviously, grape. Secondary aromas and flavors refer to smells and tastes resulting from the next stage of winemaking, malolactic fermentation (smells of "butter" or "cheese" can be identified at this level), while the tertiary level refers to the sensations resulting from bottle aging, when wine sits untouched for years. Such smells range from "orange marmalade" to "petrol."

At the bottom of Systematic Approach to Tasting handouts, there is a note to students who are studying to obtain their certification. The terms are not a panacea; "you do not need to limit yourself." Examiners will accept any words, "so long as they are accurate."

Freeing the language

About six years before Noble created the wine wheel, Robert Parker, a lawyer from Maryland, started a newsletter that used a points system to rate wines on their color and appearance, aroma, flavor, and overall quality.[18] This new form of ranking broke from previous, non-numerical criticism, and today, Parker is considered the world's most influential wine critic. His hundred point scale is ubiquitous, with detractors charging that his preference for fruity, heavy wine set a standard for what is deemed "good"—and, as a result, changed the world's palate.

Despite the objectivity rankings and tasting guides project, taste and smell are fundamentally subjective. Esther Mobley, the *San Francisco Chronicle*'s senior wine critic, wrote that conventional wine language excludes "dimensions of flavor that are unfamiliar to the white, Western cultures that dominate the world of fine wine."[19] During a conversation I had with Mobley in San Francisco, I learned that black currant, typically evoked in tasting notes for Cabernets, is illegal to grow in parts of the United States, meaning that many Americans who have never traveled abroad will not actually know what the fruit tastes like; instead, they understand black currant to taste like Cabernets, not the other way around.

Miguel de Leon, a New York-based wine professional who grew up in the Philippines, wrote for *Punch* magazine about how white and Western-oriented tasting notes can alienate non-white drinkers. He recounted trying a wine from France's Loire Valley that smelled like "the memory of my childhood wrapped up in the jackfruit of Savennières," and tasting a Cab Franc that reminded him of "the tamarind candies I used to buy in the Philippines when I was little, before I moved to America."[20] But the wine tasting sheet didn't include such flavor possibilities, nor did his white classmates engage with discussions of sensory experiences different from their own. "It feels bewildering, frustrating, lonely," he wrote of his experience.

When we discuss wine, we grasp for metaphors to communicate our experience of the drink to others. Those metaphors might have no meaning for people whose sense histories differ from our own. But the beauty of wine, I was beginning to learn in Spain, is in the multitude of meanings different people derive from its flavors. Today, in response to the white and Western standardization of wine language, young wine professionals are pushing to free the language from the confines of technical, exclusionary tasting notes. Wine, the say, should tell a story that goes beyond rote words and phrases. By sharing our sense stories, wine drinking can be more inclusive, more communal—and, ultimately, more joyful.

Over the years, friends have proffered wonderful notes on wine, observations that conjure deeply personal places and memories. The most evocative come from people who are not steeped in wine's canned language. My partner, who is from Oregon, grew up snacking on wild blackberries from the woods near his home and spent a summer living on a vineyard near Salem, picking cherries in his spare time. He once noted to me that the color of a Gamay from Beaujolais, France, looked like the chalky, sediment-rich juice collected in a cherry pitter. Another time, he compared a wine's taste to that of gummy peach rings. These observations opened conversations to our memories, the flavors of childhood.

Sense memories

By the time I spoke with Joan Gómez Pallarès at the bar in Tarragona, several months after moving to the country, my Spanish had greatly improved, and I was able to hold complete, if limited, conversations. But I still struggled to find the right words for wine in any language.

Smell, Pallarès reminded me, is the sense most deeply associated with memory. There's some speculation as to why, exactly, but in a 2021 paper from Northwestern University, scientists concluded that there's a neurological connection between the hippocampus and the brain's olfactory regions. "Nearly everyone has been transported by a whiff of an odor to another time and place, an experience that sights or sounds rarely evoke," the paper's lead investigator, Christina Zelano, said in a press release for the study.[21]

I told Pallarès about my difficulty matching words and memories to a wine's smells. "One's sense memory," he said, "is like a muscle, meant to be exercised." He suggested I visit a spice market and linger with its scents. Sumac, tarragon, coriander—I should store these things away. Everywhere else, I should keep my nose open, readying myself for the smells of the world.

Mapping scents, I realized, could help me identify flavors in the wine. Smell evoked memory, and certain memories could give me an object of comparison. If I could identify something familiar in the wine, then I'd be able to articulate what it was I smelled or tasted. Later, I'd make lists of the smells I knew. Red wine vinegar applied to my hair during summer break, to bleach out the green from pool chlorine. Vicks VapoRub, smeared on my throat and chest when I was sick. Unlike Pallarès, who'd told me that the yellow wine we were drinking had reminded him of flowers from his village, my memorable smells were not from nature. They revealed the essence of my childhood, my upbringing primarily in man-made spaces. But if I could recall enduring aromas specific to my past, I would be better equipped to identify other smells I'd smelled before, ones that were less memorable to me but still stored away somewhere in my brain. And, by training my nose in the landscapes where I lived and worked, I could create new sense memories.

I took a sip of the wine and tried to picture the land where its grapes were grown: a vineyard not too far from us, hot and dusty and twenty miles inland from the sea. After months of drinking and learning, wine became more than a means to bring me to Spain. It was a tool to help me *understand* Spain—its geography, weather, and culture. Drinking and speaking about wine was refining my senses, and, in turn, helping me assign words to my sensorial experiences. It could teach me about the natural world.

Pruning

In February, Carmen and I spent long days in the vineyard. It was pruning season, and there were two of us, sometimes three, to chop branches from thirty-thousand plants. The earth was frozen. The sky was concrete gray, big around us. A strong wind blew. On my first day, Carmen taught me how to prune a plant so it would be strong enough to hold healthy grapes. During the winter, vines contain many dormant buds, indicating where a leaf grew in the prior season and representing possible growing points for the upcoming season. If too many buds grow into shoots, the vine will develop a surplus of weak grapes with irregular sun exposure, since, instead of developing in close clusters, they spread apart on the plant. That's why she pruned—to remove excess buds and encourage vigorous, limited grape growth.

Carmen's method was called double cordon pruning, which keeps intact a horizontal extension of the vine's trunk year after year. The extension, called a cordon, is a V-shaped part of the vine that looks like shrugging shoulders. Various branches grew from the cordon, and my task was to reduce the number of branches to six. "You have to learn to read the plant," Carmen told me. "You need to know where it should grow next year."

We worked and my palms ached and the sound, the abrupt crack as the shears met the wood and the wood fell away, echoed in my head. Carmen's mother collected the branches as we went. My hands were clumsy, and I worked slowly, making mistakes. Carmen corrected me. But after hours of walking up and down the rows, I fell into a rhythm. The work was mesmerizing.

I thought of the power I wielded in dictating how the vines would grow. The moment I cut a branch, my action was irreversible. The gravity of this realization, that I could change the future of a plant—and, in turn, the harvest months from now—drew me into a sort of tunnel vision. I saw nothing but the vine in front of me. My mind felt clear, my arms strong. We stretched and bent and lifted our bodies, as if in supplication.

Sometimes Carmen would pause and comment on a single vine, beckoning me back to the present. "They remind me of humans. Human hands," she said. "Just look at them. It's like they're grasping up into the air."

I left her vineyard after pruning, on a train bound northeast, for Catalonia. It was almost spring.

SPRING

L'Albera, Vermont

L'Albera

I first saw L'Albera at night. I'd traveled north by train from Barcelona to Figueres, Salvador Dalí's hometown, and then by bus to Sant Climent Sescebes, a village of about 500 people near the French border. It was dark when I boarded the bus, and I could only make out vague shapes and silhouettes in the dim landscape around me. We wound through quiet neighborhoods, their stone buildings illuminated by weak streetlights. Passengers left the bus one by one. At the second-to-last stop, a man in army fatigues got out and disappeared into the darkness. There was, I'd been told, a military base just outside of town, and some days artillery practice could be heard across the foothills. I was headed to the last stop, farther north and east, to a forested nature reserve. It was strange, I thought, a nature reserve next to a military base: preservation and destruction adjacent.

Barbara, one of the winemakers I'd traveled to stay with for a few months, picked me up in a blue van. She had a wide smile and feathery eyebrows that reminded me of an owl's tufts, and she spoke to me in Italian-accented Spanish, a holdover from her three decades in Milan, where she was born and raised. She drove us ten minutes down a dirt road, toward the mountains. The massif of L'Albera was the easternmost extension of the Pyrenees and eventually tapered off into the Mediterranean; just beyond was France. Sweeping south from the mountains was an alluvial plain, called Empordá.[1] Dispersed across the plain were Roman-era footpaths and megalithic stone monuments called dolmens, which dated back some seven thousand years. In the foothills, Barbara said, one could sense the antiquity of the land.

Joan Carles, Barbara's husband, was sitting in the farmhouse kitchen when we arrived. It was cavernous and drafty, with a massive hearth in one corner and a gas stove next to a worn wooden table. Carles, as Barbara called him, had a low, gruff voice, and his Spanish was inflected with a northern Catalan accent that required my full attention to comprehend. After a few minutes chatting about missiles the army had accidentally lobbed into a nearby forest several years before, Barbara showed me to my room upstairs. It was spartan, with a small desk and chair, and a double bed facing a set of glass doors. The doors led to a terrace that, as I could gather despite the darkness, looked out to farmland. Settling under the sheets, I watched the night deepen until I fell asleep.

La Gutina

L'Albera was just the name of the mountain range, but I came to think of it as a region unto itself. I'd come to live here because I wanted to see a new landscape, and to apply what I had learned with Carmen to another place and season. During the springtime, Carles and Barbara spent much of the day working in the vines for their winery, Celler La Gutina. They had 80 hectares of land: vineyards, oak and chestnut forests, and olive groves interspersed with scrubland, meadows, and ponds that existed only during years of good rainfall. The river Anyet threaded through the foothills, and trails connected the region's villages. The landscape teemed with life: a diversity of plants—wild asparagus, thyme, lavender, rosemary, sage—flourished alongside javelinas, turtles, eagles, and owls. On the property lived a number of farm animals, too: five chickens, two horses, two dogs, and two donkeys. The vines themselves amounted to some seven and a half hectares, scattered in small parcels around the property, and required attention year-round.

Though the couple and I spoke in Spanish, Catalan, a more guttural language, was ubiquitous on the farms around L'Albera. *Buen día* became *bon día*; *lluvia*, rain, became *pluja*. I could barely understand Catalan, and I still struggled to talk about wine in Spanish and English. Remembering Pallarès's suggestion that I train my senses, I walked through the backcountry, plucking dry brush to smell and wild fennel to chew. Finding words to describe my reality—whether the trees in the back country or the wine I drank—seemed important to my understanding of the world. And if I could assign language to my reality, I was better equipped to share, rendering my experience of the world comprehensible to others.

Sitting in a Garnacha vineyard with Barbara one afternoon, I told her about my enduring difficulties with language—with wine's lexicon, Spanish, and now, Catalan. Around us, grapes were budding, and we admired the contrast between their bright green shoots and dark blue mountains to the north. The sun, cutting through looming rain clouds, threw a dusty gold film over the land. "I'd never known there could be so many nuances to light before I came here," Barbara said. "I'm not a fan of Dalí, but I understand his colors." She assured me that finding words takes time and intention. I realized that Barbara, like me, had grown up far from this abundance. She, too, had learned to speak.

Dirt

Barbara and Carles had met at a week-long African dance class in La Jonquera, a Catalan border town best known for being home to one of Europe's largest brothels. Barbara traveled there from Milan, where she was working as an architect. Carles was a firefighter from Figueres, learning how to play the djembe. As Carles tells it, they fell for each other immediately. But they could barely communicate with one other: Barbara didn't know Spanish or Catalan, and Carles only spoke a bit of her language, which he learned from Italians who hunted birds in the area when he was a child. Carles was also married—though separated—with four children. But after he met Barbara, he divorced his wife, and the unlikely couple began a whirlwind romance. Barbara rode her motorcycle for an entire day from Milan to visit. She took Spanish classes in Italy, then moved to Barcelona. In 2007, she moved to the farmhouse in the foothills where I was now staying.

In the mornings, I'd wake up at six and make coffee on the stovetop. We'd sit at the kitchen table, sipping and picking at bread, and Carles and Barbara would discuss the day's tasks, needling one another in the tired manner of an old couple. Carles was usually laid-back and chipper, while Barbara was anxious and fatalistic about the weather.

Theirs was the kind of home where the presence of dirt was unavoidable. It coated their boots, their pants, their hands and their hair. Windows were flung open, beckoning rain, dust, and wind. Birds darted through the cellar and nested in the rafters. One afternoon, after Carles's son killed the family rooster out of spite—it had crowed at all hours of the day—I found the carcass dangling upside down from the laundry room ceiling, blood dripping into a bucket.

Working with vines anywhere requires a profound knowledge of place. The orientation of the vineyard—whether it faces north, south, east, or west—affects the growth of the vines, as does elevation, humidity, wind patterns, and strength of sunlight. All of these factors play a subtle role in how the wine tastes.

So, too, does dirt. The type of soil changes the way grapevines grow. La Gutina had two soils: *sauló*, a sandy granite, and *llicorella*, quartz slate with layers of clay. Granite is porous, drains well, and tends to have a higher pH, and vines must grow deep into the earth to reach water. *Llicorella* reflects and conserves heat, which bolsters sugar production in grapes. Carmen told me in the winter that, counterintuitively, poor soil requires roots to dig deeper, grow stronger, and branch off in a process called "ramifying" to absorb minerals, making healthier grapes.

When rain fell, wild grasses and plants sprouted between the rows of vines. Natural winemakers were fond of telling me that there was no such thing as a *mala hierba*—a "bad plant," or weed—though they did tear up the purple blossomed malva, whose leaves provided refuge for pests and viruses. Some plants could help prevent erosion, aerate the soil, or give nitrogen to the millions of microorganisms dwelling in the dirt. In the Santa Olalla vineyard, Carmen planted herbs and small fruit trees between the vines to force competition and make each plant grow stronger, but in L'Albera, nature needn't any prodding. The vineyards, surrounded by forests and brimming with native medicinal herbs, were already plentiful.

Spring was a vulnerable season for the grapevine, the time when the plant emerged from its winter dormancy to grow shoots and buds. Two years before I arrived, Barbara and

Carles lost most of their grapes to powdery mildew, which thrives in humid weather. To stave off moisture, we spent a few days spraying vineyards with small amounts of sulfur, a practice that's generally accepted in natural wine circles. I walked up and down rows wearing goggles and a mask, a heavy canister of sulfur strapped to my back. Other days, Barbara and I plucked extraneous leaves to help aerate the plants, blaring Latin American rock music from our phones.

After breakfast one morning, Carles instructed me to stand on a tractor cart, ankle-deep in manure and compost, and shovel the mixture onto young vines so they'd grow stronger. He drove fast, and I had to shovel quickly. "Do you surf?" Carles asked. He jolted the tractor forward and I fell hands-first into the pile. "I thought you were from California."

One Sunday, my day off from vineyard work, I came downstairs to the kitchen to see Carles leaning over the stove, stirring onions into a cast iron for a soffritto to serve his firefighter crew, who were coming over for lunch. I laced up my sneakers to go on a walk. "Have you been to the fountain in the woods?" he asked. I shook my head. "Have you seen the century-old olive trees?" he asked. "I haven't been," I said. He frowned theatrically, his eyes teasing. "Tienes que *estar más*," he said. *You have to* be *more*.

Carles knew the land's every hill and depression. Over breakfast one day, he told me what he knew about his olive grove. "There are some magnificent trees," he told me. "I am not sure why. That's the grand mystery. Of course, the land there is good. But some years, the trees give a lot of fruit, and other years they don't. It could be because of their position with the sun, or the rain, or the humidity. It all depends on the flower, too. There are some trees whose flowers are open longer, leaving them vulnerable to the wind and the rain. The flower is nothing spectacular. Small, white. If you're not paying attention, you don't notice it."

He spent his childhood visiting the land where La Gutina was now located, which his great-grandfather had bought in the late 1800s. Years after that purchase, Carles's father planted vines to sell wine in bulk. But he abandoned the project when the business was no longer profitable. "A shame," Carles said. "He tore up most of the vines." In 2006, Carles moved to the property in the hopes of recuperating the old winery.

He loved dirt. One day, I found Carles steering the tractor toward the river, planning to dig up soil from the banks. He was looking for good dirt to grow new vines. Another time, when we were walking back to the farmhouse, he told me of a woman he'd met years ago, who smelled like soil. He fell in love with her briefly because of that—because she reminded him of the earth.

Soil geology

A soil's physical characteristics, including pH, drainage, salinity, and particle size, can affect the quality of wine.[2] Especially important to wine quality are microbiota. Each type of soil—and there are a dozen taxonomical orders, with thousands of different variations—contains different microorganisms, including yeasts, bacteria, and fungi, that break down organic material.

Scientists have extensively studied the role of microbiota in the cellar side of winemaking. Yeast on grape skins convert sugars into alcohol, and, in a secondary process known as malolactic fermentation, bacteria convert tart malic acid into softer lactic acid, making red wines (and some whites) smoother and creamier, as opposed to sharp and acidic. But beyond the cellar, studies have shown that microbiota living in vineyard soil also shape the way a wine tastes. Bacteria and fungi contribute to the health of soil, which, in turn, makes grape vines healthier. Their various other impacts, especially on soil acidity and moisture, change the way a grapevine matures.

Current soil conditions around the world stem from ancient geological events. In Washington and Oregon, Ice Age floods from Lake Missoula, Montana, swept through the Columbia River Gorge, leaving behind deposits of silt and sand.[3] Millenia worth of eruptions from Mount Etna, an active volcano on the east coast of Sicily, spewed lava, pumice, and ash, which hardened and eroded together into a sandy soil rich in potassium.[4] In southern France's Rhône region, melting glaciers deposited sediment from the Alps onto bedrock, which is now covered in sand and clay.[5]

"The best place to taste difference in terroir is the Willamette Valley because we have three major soil types," Portland State University geologist Scott Burns told me after I'd reached out to learn more about soil. "The flavors are completely different." The Willamette Valley is a fertile agricultural region bound by Oregon's Coast Range to the west and Cascade Range to the east, and its three main soils are volcanic, sedimentary, and silty. Pinot Noir, the region's famed grape, has thin skins, making it especially susceptible to environmental influence. Pinot Noirs from grapes grown in volcanic Jory soils, which are derived from the igneous Columbia River basalt, tend to be lighter in color and taste of red berries, such as raspberries and cherries, Burns said. Grapes grown in Willakenzie, a soil formed from loose loamy sandstone that drains well, tend to produce dark, strong wines that taste of blackberries and plums.[6]

Pallarès told me that whenever he visits a vineyard, he picks rocks from the earth and licks them to understand how the soil influences a wine's flavor. Following his lead, I took a small granite rock from underneath the shade of an oak tree near La Gutina's Garnacha vineyard. It tasted like dirt.

Vernatxa

Sometimes, it felt as though I was on a wine pilgrimage, collecting stories about the land like relics. I traveled south and west of L'Albera, meeting winemakers to learn about their land's history. Salvador Battle, whose wines were known across Catalonia for their acidity, was a 36-year old separatist who believed Catalonia should be independent from the rest of Spain. While taking me through his vineyards around Agullana, Salvador pointed out sagging structures built into the hillsides and told me that during the Spanish Civil War, Spain's Republican leaders fled to this town in Pyrenees, a last gasp at governing before seeking exile over the mountains in France. In Garraf, a village a few miles inland from the Mediterranean, Manel Avinyó and his daughter, Núria, known for their sparkling wines, led me around a stone farmhouse that dated back to the fourteenth century; their land, too, bore witness to Spain's long history of strife.

Francesc Ferré, a thirty-year-old winemaker, drove me through Terra Alta, a mountainous region four hours south and inland of L'Albera. Terra Alta, which means "elevated land," is thought to have inspired Pablo Picasso's cubism; the painter had convalesced in the region after a bout of sickness as a teenager. Spain's great river, the Ebro, flows just east of Terra Alta, emptying out in the Mediterranean Sea. As we drove into Francesc's hometown, Corbera d'Ebre, a weathered white stone church rose from a hill, its ruinous facade one reminder that the town was razed to the ground eighty years ago during the Spanish Civil War. In 1938, Franco's forces, aided by the Nazis, bombarded the town during the Battle of the Ebro. It was the war's longest battle.[7] Townspeople fled, and by the end of the war, when Franco's forces had won, Corbera was rubble. Eventually, townspeople built a new village below the ruins. Ferré's great-grandparents returned, and the family began farming grapes and olives again, as they had been doing for centuries.

Francesc grew up in the shadow of the old village. He wanted to make wine in homage to its history, and thus, used grapes native to the region, primarily Garnacha—known, in Terra Alta's Catalan dialect, as "Vernatxa." He also revived old winemaking techniques, such as the skin contact white grape fermentation and barrel aging of "vinos brisants." "The most interesting thing about a wine," Francesc told me in his cellar as we drank a heavy, mineral white Vernatxa, "is where it comes from, what history it carries."

Everything about the land was steeped in history. His vines were grown in clay and *panal,* a sandy soil formed by the fossils of sea creatures, and some were a hundred years old. Francesc drove me to a massive olive tree called Lo Parot, its trunk wide and gnarled. Lo Parot, he told me, was 2,000 years old, its lifespan dating back to the Romans. Winemaking in the region is thought to date back even longer, to the Iberians. Today, Francesc hosts wine tastings near the hilltop site of a Civil War trench. He still finds shrapnel in the hills.

Payés

Montse Molla, 35, was the first female winemaker in her town, Calonge, on Catalonia's Costa Brava. When I arrived at the 700-year-old winery for a visit, Montse was out in an orchard; the Mollas cultivated fruit trees and vegetables, which they sold at local markets, as was custom of traditional payés (peasant farmer) families.

Montse brought me to her musty cellar, where weathered wooden barrels lined the stone walls. She told me that locals drank her wine in search of a hazy reunion with neighborhood memories. And she knew the old style well. Montse made wine called "vino de payés," a modest natural wine made the way her family had been doing it for more than a century. Each barrel, she told me, is different. Many of her customers—who were predominately Catalan, from the Costa Brava—prefer her "polvos," the bottles of sparkling wine that accumulated layers of dust while sitting in the dark cellar. They wanted to drink something that dredged up memories, something that brought to mind mid-afternoons sitting with their grandmothers at the kitchen table, eating wine-soaked bread drizzled with sugar, as was common half a century ago.

For decades, writers and sommeliers referred to six "noble" grape varieties: Cabernet Sauvignon, Merlot, Pinot Noir, Chardonnay, Sauvignon Blanc, and Riesling. Most are French, and the last, Riesling, comes from Germany. Assigning grape varieties the status of nobility is in line with other practices in the world of prestige wine. In Bordeaux, for example, wineries are ranked by a classification system created in 1855 by French Emperor Napoleon III; "premier cru" refers to the highest quality of wines—and the most expensive.[8]

There are, in fact, at least 1,300 wine grape varieties, if not thousands more.[9] As a way to reclaim their heritage, Catalan winemakers like Montse prefer using indigenous grapes such as Garnatxa Roja and Sumoll, and traditional vinification methods. They farmed land that had been in their families for generations, an accumulation of wealth and property I didn't often see in vineyards outside of Europe, and told variations on one story: I was once a child here. My parents were once children here. We've always been here. It seemed like everyone had a story of a grandfather working the vines. This is one way of being Catalan—spending centuries on the same land.

Tramuntana

In late spring in L'Albera, a blistering wind blew. It rocked the house, howling down the chimney. Outdoors, the wind screamed. The wind was called the Tramuntana, Catalan for "across the mountains," and it blew south from France, over the Pyrenees, at random intervals throughout the year, though usually in the spring and winter. The Tramuntana was so powerful it reshaped the landscape. Thin pines growing on seaside cliffs bent so far south they were nearly horizontal, making coastal cities appear permanently windswept. In the sky, the wind elongated clouds into the shape of serpents. Cows, Carles told me, sometimes fell into the river and disappeared during the Tramuntana. He said people went mad when it blew.

The air had an electric energy those days. At night, I walked through the vineyards, hair whipping across my face, and felt like I had enough power to stay awake for days. I remembered California's Santa Ana winds, which marked the start of fire season when I was growing up—one of the few reference points reminding me that my home was, indeed, part of the natural world.

Vineyard work became more strenuous and methodical. When she saw the forecast, Barbara, worried about the health of budding vines, decided that our next task was urgent. One morning, we rushed through the vineyards with string to tie the plants' limbs together. By making the leaves and branches more compact, Barbara hoped the vines would be shielded from the wind's destruction. The vines were just weeks away from flowering, and counter-measures were essential to the survival of future grapes.

Carles, meanwhile, wanted to plant a new vineyard. We were to graft four hundred Garnacha Gris vines to American rootstock while the Tramuntana blew dust and debris at our faces. There were six of us to plant: me; Carles and Barbara; 70-year-old Andalucían brothers named José and Antonio; and a seasonal worker from Gambia named Idreesa, whom they hired on a project-by-project basis throughout the year.

To start, Barabara, Carles, or José would slice open a piece of already-planted rootstalk, then wedge into the opening a small slat of vine resembling a clarinet reed. Carles hammered sharp pieces of cane, which I had cut into spears the day before, next to the vines for support. Carles called me the *enterradora*, the digger; I was responsible for covering the newly grafted vines with fresh soil so they wouldn't wither. The winds, however, had dried the soil into a hard crust. My bones prickled each time the shovel's blade struck. My hands ached.

José, the older of the brothers, taught me how to dig. How to stand with my feet planted behind the root and scrape the dry earth in a circular motion, how to drag the pile of loose dirt inward toward the plant. He shouted over the wind, "You shouldn't dig so close to the root, otherwise you'll damage it. Don't bend over so much." The instructions were mortifying, a reminder of my estrangement from the earth. I tucked my chin to hide my face from the wind, but that made my digging clumsier. José took the shovel from my hands and showed me.

That Barbara worked at all became the joke of the week. For much of history, women were excluded from winemaking work entirely. In her 2006 book *Women of Wine*, Ann B. Matasar explained that at the time of her writing, some male winemakers in France still thought menstruation would spoil fermenting wine, so women were barred from the cellar.[10] Men thought women's frail bodies would not exert the proper amount of force to extract juice, so they were prohibited from stomping on grapes. Instead, when men were finished with the day's work, women would make them lunch.

"Barbara shouldn't be out here," joked José. "Where are the heels?" Barbara was wearing dirty pants and mud-caked boots as she cut through rootstalk. "You should be sitting with your heels on the Rambla of Figueres, drinking a beer, passing the day."

Barbara kept up the joke for the next few days. "Forgot my heels this morning!" she yelled, kneeling in the dirt. "Now all I need are my heels and I can go dancing," she said another time, after José fashioned her a skirt of vine branches to protect her lower back from the sun. The jokes were light-hearted, but within them I sensed an uneasy truth: even in 2018, women winemakers were rare in Spain. I'd hardly seen any women working outside in L'Albera at all.

Renaissance des Appellations

One weekend, I took a train to Barcelona to help Carmen present her wines at the Renaissance des Appellations fair, held in the city's regal maritime museum. The annual event showcases wines from dozens of winemakers around the world, all of whom farm biodynamically. Biodynamic farming is a style of holistic agriculture developed by Rudolf Steiner, a nineteenth-century Austrian philosopher and mystic who was interested in the connection between the spiritual and the physical worlds. Central to biodynamics is the notion that an entire farm—or, in Carmen's case, an entire vineyard— is a single organism. The goal of biodynamic farmers is to maintain equilibrium between plants, animals, humans, and the soil by nurturing biodiversity through cover crops, usually wild plants that help maintain soil health (which conventional winemakers often consider weeds), and polyculture, the introduction of other plants and herbs into the vineyard. To foster the growth of healthy bacteria and fungi, farmers create biodynamic compost with "preparations" from medicinal herbs like yarrow, chamomile, stinging nettle, dandelion, oak bark, and valerian. The movement's most adherent followers bury, and then unearth, cow horns full of manure to make sprays they believe will strengthen vineyard soil, and follow the lunar calendar to determine when to perform certain tasks, such as planting vines or bottling wine.[11]

Carmen and I set up her table in the sunlit event room and placed bottles of red wine on ice so they wouldn't overheat. When the fair began, wine professionals—including sommeliers, importers, distributors, and restaurant owners—streamed into the space, clutching glasses. Carmen was friendly and informative, talking with tasters about her winemaking methods: *suelo arcilloso-calcáreo; clima de extremos; un año en depósito de acero inoxidable.* Clay and limestone soil, extreme climate, one year in a stainless steel deposit. After a few hours, she had to drive back to Torrijos, more than four hundred miles away. "Defend the wine," Carmen told me, and I was alone.

A wide spectrum of men came to taste Carmen's wine that afternoon. I met a giddy sommelier-in-training who raised his wine glass above his head, rather theatrically, to comment on the depth and nuances of the wine's color. I met a flannel-wearing man who turned to his wife and repeated everything I said, as though his words made more sense or his wife didn't understand. I met men in business attire who spit out their wine after tasting; a backpacked tourist dad with three children in tow; a man in a white tank top who held his glass aggressively, with a clenched fist; several slim, bespectacled men quietly taking notes on the soil's characteristics; and tan winemakers, parched and bored from repeating the same talking points to hundreds of tasters. Every so often, they slinked over to my table to drink a little for themselves.

I was pouring too much wine into people's glasses, I learned, when a shocked woman shouted, "That is quite enough!" One man approached the table, and, looking from my face to the winery's name—Uva de Vida—said, "You're not from here, are you?" to which I replied in my accented Spanish, "What made you guess?" When I asked another man if he'd like to try Carmen's wine, he eyed her bottles, crossed his arms, and frowned like a toad. "Convince me," he said. I poured. He took a sip, then walked away with no further comment.

In the evening, a man who seemed to be in his late fifties approached my table. His unbrushed gray hair stuck to the sweat on his forehead. He wore a wrinkled polo shirt tucked into khakis over a sagging beer belly and donned a watch on his wrist but checked the time with his cellphone. He did not take notes, nor did he raise his glass toward the overhead lights.

I offered him my memorized speech, with the caveat that I was not the winemaker: *We're based in Toledo, a 14-hectare vineyard with Graciano and Tempranillo, soil is clay and limestone. Five hundred meters altitude, extreme climate, little precipitation.*

He sipped, cringed, and sweated. His face grew red. Carmen's wines were high in alcohol and best suited for a dinner of stew in the wintertime; though I loved drinking them, they were less appealing in hot, stuffy rooms. "I know Graciano," the man said. "When the Graciano is done well, it is acidic and fresh. This wine . . . It can't be saved. It just can't be saved."

I wondered if Carmen would be ashamed of me. I was not heeding her command to defend the wine. The man asked about maceration with grape skins. He asked about the level of volatility. He asked about the grams of residual sugars. "I'm sorry," I said. "I don't know."

Taste and power

Acidity, residual sugar—knowing these things feels powerful. So does knowing about the land, about its rocks and soil, its wind patterns, its slopes. They're two different but related epistemologies of wine: the structural and the ecological, the first primarily stemming from cellar work and the second from vineyard work. In the social world of wine drinking, the pursuit of that first set of knowledge has spawned a culture of performativity, one that often suggests certain people are more authoritative than others.

In the special collections room at the University of California, Davis library, I read a headline in the *Chicago Tribune*: "Do Wines Make Women Giggly?"[12] The writer, Ruth Ellen Church, was an approachable yet incisive critic and the first person to pen a wine column in a major American newspaper. In her column "Let's Learn About Wines," she aimed to demystify the drink for her readers, suggesting pairings for Thanksgiving, explaining different wine styles, and recounting tales of casual sexism in the industry. This particular piece, from 1965, began with an anecdote about a "member of several gastronomical societies" who claimed dining clubs wouldn't open their membership to women because they "'don't know how to drink wine. They take too much and get giggly.'" In another piece, Church wrote that wine "has always been man's exclusive field of scholarship and enjoyment. If a woman appreciated wine, it was usually because her husband or lover permitted her a glass while serving as an audience for his philosophical discussions of what was in it."[13]

Church was writing more than half a century ago, but these stories of doubt cast on women's expertise resonate today. When Esther Mobley was offered the *San Francisco Chronicle*'s wine critic job in 2015, Charles Olken, a wine reviewer in northern California, expressed skepticism. "There is a raft of others out there who could have also brought the wisdom of experience to the job," he wrote in a post on his website. "Miss Mobley does not."[14] By the time she started working at the *Chronicle*, Mobley had been an assistant editor at *Wine Spectator*, a major wine magazine, and had worked harvests in North and South America. (Olken, meanwhile, spelled her name incorrectly and gotten her age wrong.)

In 2021, Kryss Speegle, a San Francisco Bay Area based winemaker and sales professional, was named a Master of Wine, one of the industry's most prestigious titles, after passing a rigorous theory and tasting examination. A previous job had her working and giving tours at a winery in northern California. During a tour, a man in the group asked, "Do the winemakers let you taste the wines?" He then asked to speak with a winemaker. When Speegle responded that *she* was one of the winemakers, he was clearly surprised.

In her twenty years working in the industry, Speegle has also noticed how wine professionals tend to patronize certain customers for their presumed tastes. People who drink sweet wines are often considered "bottom shelf consumers," as are people who drink wine with Coca Cola, Speegle said.

It's a reductive stereotype, meanwhile, to assume women only like light or sweet white wines, and that men like complex, heavy, oaky reds—stereotypes often found in wine tasting notes, too. In his 2012 book *The Juice: Vinous Veritas*, writer Jay McInerney described one wine as "a youthful and powerful beauty like Milla Jovovich in Resident Evil," and a different wine as "more voluptuous and decadent, with a honeyed quality that put me in mind of Ava Gardner in

The Barefoot Contessa."[15] In another part of the book, he wrote that some Australians refer to certain shiraz wines as "leg spreaders," letting the crude language speak for itself. "However, given the sheer size and power of these behemoths," he continued, "stereotypically masculine metaphors seem more appropriate to me; high-octane potions like Kaesler's Old Bastard Shiraz remind me more of a muscle car like a Dodge Charger or a Viper than of a starlet, more of Russell Crowe than Naomi Watts."[16]

Taste is not innate, nor is it sacred. It's learned, based on our sensory experiences—the food we ate growing up, and the drinks we try as adults. "No one comes out of the womb drinking wine," Speegle told me. As anthropologist Sidney Mintz wrote in *Sweetness and Power*, taste is bound up in class dynamics; to have "good taste" is often a signifier of wealth, and once a certain commodity becomes accessible to lower classes—as is the case with sugar, Mintz's focus—it loses its exclusionary power.[17] Once the rich can no longer distinguish themselves from the poor based on what they consume, they consume something else.

Killing the Bull

As spring stretched longer and warmer in L'Albera, I saw the landscape change—slowly at first and then quickly, the progression of time manifest in the world around me. Grain fields turned a tropical green. Mountains became indigo.

Hills transformed to electric yellow, suddenly alight with wildflowers. I'd never really noticed seasonal changes before, but outside every day, time slowed, accentuating even the subtlest shifts in the environment.

It rained often, and the evenings were humid. On sleepless nights, I could feel every mattress coil dig into my back. I dragged a blanket and pillow to the terrace and slept in the moonlight. In the morning I found leaves in my hair. One night, a mosquito droned in my ear. I battled the mosquito, the insect circling closer, me swatting. I tired myself, and the next morning I woke with swollen eyelids from where the mosquito had bitten me. At the breakfast table, Carles rolled cigarettes and laughed. Barbara told me to go into the fields and find wild thyme, make an infusion, and press a damp cloth against my eyelids. The herb, she said, was anti-inflammatory. It worked.

A herd of wild cows began occupying the hills to the northeast. "Do you see them?" Carles asked, pointing while we worked. I squinted. I'd thought the black-and-white shapes were boulders, but now I could see they were moving. A quarter of a century ago, Carles told me, a group of cows escaped from a property in the hills and, over the years, grew into a wild herd. Now, some fifty cows roamed the region untethered, devouring crops and sowing general chaos. If the cows came to the valley, Carles said, he'd shoot one, carve it up, and freeze its meat. "There's nothing like a strong, untreated bull," he told me.

A few days later, Barbara announced that Carles had killed a bull. He'd spotted it grazing in a meadow, returned to the house for a rifle, and shot it in the head. I hurried to the meadow, where the black bull's body lay stiff in a field of grass and white blossoms. Its legs were stick straight, and a bright ribbon of blood circled its neck. Carles, his son, and two friends—an Argentinian butcher and a Catalan chef—were gathered around the carcass, strategizing. The butcher, who wore red rain boots, bent over the bull holding a knife. With swift movements, he skinned the creature and sliced its belly open. Foul-smelling fluids and blood spilled onto the grass. Next, he cut out the organs: the stomach, liver, lungs, and heart. He cut off the cow's lower legs and hooves, and, with a saw, cut off the head. Using a tree branch, the butcher devised a pulley system to lift the carcass into the back of a truck. He drove the carcass to the house, where he continued cutting and cleaning for the rest of the afternoon. As he worked, Perla, Barbara's elegant, blue-eyed border collie, gnawed on a hoof. A few days later, we dined on bull burgers with a side of french fries.

Antifreeze

In recent years, springtime has been an anxious season for European winemakers. April of 2022 saw a record-breaking cold spell that threatened vineyards in France and Spain.[18] The winter was warm, and by April the buds had already opened, making them especially vulnerable to damage. Vines were covered in ice, and, in some places the temperature was

23 degrees Fahrenheit, some 20 to 30 degrees colder than normal.[19] To mitigate the damage, farmers lit large antifreeze candles, which helps prevent heat loss by forming a blanket of smoke over the vines. They started up wind machines to pull warm air from high above a field down closer to the vines. They burned bales of hay among the vines—anything to protect their vines from frost.

For the past five years, drastic climate events—frost, hail, unseasonable cold and rain—have destroyed crops and put farmers in economic peril. The Jura, a small region in eastern France along the Swiss border, usually has cold winters and dry, warm summers, but recently, hotter winter temperatures have caused earlier bud breaks. The bud break is a pivotal event in viticulture, harkening the emergence of green shoots from which leaves, stems, and grapes will eventually grow. But when buds open up too early, they are left vulnerable to the elements. In 2021, springtime frost ravaged grapevines, destroying shoots and, with them, the possibility of future grape growth. In addition to hail in June and a rainy, cool summer that brought disease and rot to vineyards, the frost drastically reduced wine production by around 30 percent on average across the country, with some winegrowers experiencing even more damage.[20] The tumultuous weather led to some $2.4 billion in losses for French vineyards.

Climate change has taken a psychic toll on winemakers, too. Jura has become something of a cult region for natural wine lovers; demand is high for Jura wine, putting the pressure on winemakers to produce more bottles than is actually possible given their lower yields. In 2021, at least four French winemakers, including one from Jura, died by suicide. While each circumstance is unique, their deaths appear to be part of a suicide epidemic among French farmers, driven to some extent by the economic havoc wreaked by climate change. One French farmer took his or her life every two days, according to a 2018 report by Public Health France, and the rate of suicide among farmers is 20 percent higher than the rate among French people as a whole.[21]

Love work mountain

When, in early June 2022, I told friends I was driving to Vermont to visit a winemaker, some seemed puzzled. *Wine in Vermont? Isn't it too cold?* But as the world's climate becomes more volatile, winemakers are planting hybrid grape varieties in regions once seen as inhospitable to viticulture. Such grapes, a result of cross-breeding between the common grapevine *Vitis vinifera* and indigenous American vines, are more resistant to fungal infection and capable of withstanding freezing temperatures. Deirdre Heekin, the winemaker I visited, was an early champion of hybrid grapes in Vermont. For the past twenty years, she has been making bright, acidic wines from these cold-hardy grapes, often co-fermenting the grapes with apples. Deirdre believes that, with an increasingly erratic climate, resilient hybrid grapes are the future.

I began my drive to Bethel, Vermont, in a torrential downpour, but by the time I crossed over the White River, the rain had lightened to a drizzle. I inched my rental car along the muddy road winding up Mount Hunger, driving slowly enough to notice purple lupines sprouting from the thick grass. Beech and birch woods gave way to wide meadows and vistas of rolling hills, fog hanging between peaks.

Inside the farmhouse, a humble wooden home crammed with wine bottles and stacks of books, Deirdre poured a glass of her 2020 wine Love Work Mountain, a sparkling red made from Marquette and La Crescent, grapes hybridized by scientists from the University of Minnesota, a grape breeding program that formally launched in the mid-1980s. Like any crop breeding program, the University of Minnesota aims to identify and isolate the genes in wild vines best suited to withstand harsh environments. In the case of Frontenac, a hybrid red grape Deirdre grows in her vineyards, scientists found what would become its American parent growing wild near a small town outside of Minneapolis. The vine, *Vitis riparia*, could survive in environments as cold as negative 33 degrees Fahrenheit.[22] Both Marquette and La Crescent have more complex ancestries, descending from other hybrids and European grapes: Pinot Noir for Marquette, and various Muscats for La Crescent.

As we sipped and chatted, Camila Carrillo—the assistant winegrower for Deirdre's winery, La garagista, and the grower behind the label La Montañuela—burst into the living room, her Australian shepherd Blue bounding in behind her. "It was a hurricane out there," she sighed. She'd driven from her home in the Lake Champlain Valley, an hour and a half away, where Deirdre also had a few vineyard plots. The Lake Champlain Valley was hotter and drier than the cooler, rainier Mount Hunger, meaning that those grapes usually matured sooner than the grapes next to Deirdre's house. But climate change is altering much about the growing season. "Ripening schedules used to be very different and now they're moving closer and closer together," Deirdre told me. "There used to be a month between blossoming. We used to pick these vineyards no earlier than mid-October," she continued, referring to the grapes we could see out the front window. "The past two years, we've had to start picking in September here."

Caleb, Deirdre's husband and co-owner of the winery, laid out a lunch of sweet potato soup and cilantro, salad with radishes from the garden, and lemon chicken cutlets. Sitting down to eat, Deirdre enumerated other ways that climate change is re-shaping her vineyards. Normally, insects die during the winter, but now, warmer temperatures are keeping them alive longer. Unseasonal rain during harvest threatens to dilute grapes. "Weather is causing bird migration to change and we're getting birds at the wrong time, and they're hungry," Deirdre added. During Hurricane Florence, Caleb said, migratory birds who would have otherwise left Vermont before grape ripening held back, waiting for the winds down south to abate. "Overnight, the vineyard was stripped," Deirdre said. "We could make no wine from that plot."

When the sun broke through, clouds parting to reveal a brilliant blue sky, we brought our conversation the vineyard. A brook gargled below the rows of vines and apple orchards. The ground squished, and long wild grass soaked our boots. Deirdre pointed out native plants growing beneath the vines. Each, she said, had anti-fungal and microbial properties that improved grape health. There was golden rod, bishop's weed, wild fern. "Ferns tell us that we should probably do an application of compost. Or, having sheep graze will help with manure and urine," Deirdre said. "The soil must be acidic for it to be friendly for ferns." Clovers, she added, pointing to a low-growing bunch, extract nitrogen from the air and bring it into the soil.

"All these plants are indicators," she said. "We had an outbreak of Japanese beetles one year and there was a new plant growing. It was a wild chrysanthemum. Turns out both the organic and synthetic sprays for Japanese beetles are made with a base of wild chrysanthemum. It was like, wow, the vineyard offered that up because it knew."

This idea is powerful: The vineyard is sentient and knows what it needs to grow healthy and strong. To be a winegrower—the term Deirdre prefers for her vocation—is to humble oneself, and to return to uninhibited communion with the world. To do so is to accept that there is much to learn from the non-human life around us.

As we cut along a path below the vines to return to the house, a flash of black shot up from the grass, a flurry of flapping wings. Blue lurched forward, growling, and Deirdre lunged to hold her back. We looked to the ground. A cluster of tiny grouse chicks huddled tight next to one another, beady eyes peering up at the humans who'd disturbed their peace.

Mildew

Late spring in L'Albera was contradictory. Meteorologists forecasted afternoon sun; instead, liters of cold rain pounded the earth. The mornings when sun wasn't supposed to come, it blazed with a neck-reddening heat and vanished by the evening as thunderstorms rolled in. The sky was often a haze, like a lens fogged by heavy breathing. This humid weather was a source of great stress. Unlike in the earlier spring, when Barbara's method of tying vines with string had protected the plants against the Tramuntana, she now hoped for wind—any wind. But the wind did not come.

Most of the vines we'd planted during the Tramuntana had died. Carles had taken a grafting course and somehow got it in his head that, to prevent fungal infection, he should boil the shoots before grafting them to the rootstock. The boiling surely killed them, we surmised by June, when the vines should have sprouted green but instead remained lifeless wood. Some time later, I learned the word *enterradora* usually refers to a gravedigger.

Every morning, Barbara would recite the forecast with dismay. Every afternoon, she would search her vines for the white stain of mildew on the front side of the grape leaf. In May, grape flowers perfumed the air with the smell of soap and the sea. I left their home for the summertime. No mildew yet.

SUMMER

Traveling, Catalonia

Vigo

Grapes started growing, lime green and hard as pebbles. On some of her vineyards, Barbara cut back the vines' leaves to expose grapes to the sun so they'd mature faster. Carmen kept her grapes shielded from the light, worried the skins might burn. The days were long, hot, and dry. Soon, the summertime heat would trigger ripening. I decided to travel over the summer, so I received vineyard updates only through photos.

A friend joined me in Galicia, a rainy, lush region in western Spain. I'd never been there before, but I'd heard stories of the Costa da Morte, where fishermen called *percebeiros* scuttled down cliffs, braving forty-foot waves to dislodge shellfish from rock. I also knew of the region's acidic Albariño grapes, and the Camino de Santiago, the series of old Christian pilgrimage paths that lead to a cathedral where St. James's remains are said to be buried.

My friend and I were in a city called Vigo. The water was tranquil there, and we spent afternoons on the beaches, swimming far into the Atlantic. One day, at a popular beach framed by skinny pine trees, we climbed barefoot through large clusters of granite rocks. Climbing always stirs in me a childlike urge to keep going until the earth falls away, until I've reached the mountain peak, until I've reached the tallest branch, and on this climb, we wanted to reach the tip of the rock cluster, the mass that jutted farthest into the ocean. But as we scrambled, we encountered a naked man hidden in the rocks, sunbathing. His entire body was tan and leathery, and he leaned with his back against a rock completely still, as though melded to the granite. We turned away. Trying a different path through the rocks, we encountered another naked man, and another. I suggested we return to the beach.

Late that afternoon, we walked to a bar and sat down at a plastic table a few meters from the sand. We were parched, salty, and sunburnt, in need of shade. We ordered beers. Two men at a nearby table took notice of us and sat down, one next to my friend and the other next to me. They were Gallego—from Galicia—and spoke the language, which sounds similar to Portuguese. Some say Gallego has the cadence of song; I thought it sounded melancholic. The man to my left was a carpenter at least a decade older than us. His voice was raspy, perhaps a smoker's. He had bulging eyes and a long body, like a salamander. They ordered us another round of beers. As he gave me a glass, Salamander's hand hovered over my shoulder. I moved my chair away from him, plastic scratching cement. He told me of a coastal hiking trail that connected the region's lighthouses. He said a new word, *acantilado*. Cliff. I asked questions about the percebeiros in the north, and the ocean's deadly currents. Questions allowed me to keep the conversation at a distance.

They ordered us another round of beers. By now, my thoughts were becoming hazy, and the sun was going down. Salamander kissed my cheek. I tensed. He asked me to go down to the water with him. "I need to use the restroom," I said, and I took my friend by the hand, wobbling as I walked. The bathroom smelled of beer and urine. In the dim light by the sink I began to cry. The drinks, the brain fog, the men I did not know—everything dredged up memories from years before, nights when I'd had too much to drink and men noticed. "We have to leave," I said. Back at the table, Salamander again kissed my cheek, this time damp from tears, and I told him we were leaving. It was now late and there were no taxis. The men offered to drive us to our hostel, and the friend took the wheel, drifting between lanes, swerving slightly as he turned corners. They dropped us at the curb and were gone. My head hurt. From the beer, sun, dehydration, crying, I didn't know. Nothing had happened, but I needed a shower. My skin was a stranger's. That was the beginning of summer.

Morality

Growing up, there was rarely alcohol in my house. This was strange to me; my friends' parents all drank in front of us. But my mother never touched it. Neither did my grandmother; the Church of Christ strictly prohibited social drinking. I was raised Methodist, and though the denomination isn't particularly strict with alcohol, my family's understanding of religion created an unspoken moral code in our household. No cursing. No drinking.

Sometimes my father drank beer at friends' barbecues, but I never saw him drink elsewhere. My grandfather was the only adult who drank regularly in front of me, and only at his house in the mountains—a Pabst Blue Ribbon at the kitchen table with lunch or while watching baseball games on television. When I told him that he seemed to enjoy beer, he quit drinking for a year, out of guilt, I later learned.

We didn't openly talk about alcohol with one another, so I couldn't grasp why few people in my family seemed to drink it. But I did gather that alcohol was imbued with moral significance. It would take me years to understand why.

Blackout

For eighteenth and nineteenth century evangelical preachers, the moral significance of alcohol was clear. During the

Second Great Awakening in the United States, preachers lectured on the evils of drunkenness, which, they argued, caused people to lose their faith. In his sermon "The Fatal Effects of Ardent Spirits," minister Ebenezer Porter blamed alcohol for a variety of social ills, including homelessness and criminality, and for turning men into "contemptible drones."[1] In England, some seventy years earlier, John Wesley, founder of the Methodist Church, wrote in his essay "A Word to a Drunkard" that alcohol made men "beasts" by stripping them of reason and understanding.[2]

When I was in college, my mother opened up to me about alcohol. Drinking, she said, made people embarrass themselves, and she disliked any place and occasion in which drinking was the central activity. She loathed, too, the smell of alcohol on breath. Because drinking was not welcome in our house, my father, I learned, had made a ritual of going to a local pizza parlor, ordering a pint of beer, and watching sports alone. He hid alcohol around the house and drank when no one was around.

In college, I initially avoided alcohol. Even though I lived far from my parents, I still perceived drinking as taboo. Instead of going to parties, I studied in my dorm room, disgusted yet curious as I heard my hall-mates stumbling up and down the stairs on weekend nights. I'd long stopped going to church, but some vestige of Christian morality kept me from drinking, just as I'd promised myself I wouldn't have sex until marriage. Even if I wasn't sure about God, I was sure about goodness.

But college social life revolved around drinking, and, thousands of miles away from home, I was lonely, so I started going to parties. As the only sober person in attendance, I felt awkward and self-conscious. In the late winter, I suggested to my roommate that we might drink together sometime—and we did, that March, in Central Park. Prosecco in plastic cups.

After that first taste, I drank frequently—in dorm rooms, at fraternities, at our student newspaper office. And I drank a lot: I'd wake up groggy with a searing headache and a constellation of bruises across my legs and arms. Guilt occasionally tugged at me after long nights. I was certain I'd made a fool of myself, and that my peers would judge me. Sometimes, that guilt seemed inherently Christian. I'd swung from abstinence to indulgence.

I drank more when I traveled to Europe the summer after my first year in college. I was writing for a student travel guide, and one of my assignments was to review nightlife in cities throughout southern Spain and Portugal. Most nights, I visited a bar or two, and every few nights I'd go to a club, dark and thrumming with music. Those nights would start at midnight and last six or seven hours. Because no one had ever taught me how to drink, I wasn't aware that alcohol doesn't hit the bloodstream immediately, that not eating before a night out can be dangerous. I drank mojitos and tequila and tinto de verano. I drank red wine. I blacked out on more than one occasion. One night, two of my hostel mates dropped a handle of vodka from our balcony, and it shattered on the sidewalk of one of Madrid's busiest boulevards. Thankfully no one was hurt. Another night, bent over and bleary-eyed after a long pub crawl, I was lost for hours in the city center.

Women, Bodies

For much of history, to be drunk as a woman was to be promiscuous, treacherous. "The kiss," wrote Ruth Ellen Church in one of her *Chicago Tribune* columns, "is supposed to have been invented as a means for a man to learn whether or not his lady had been into the wine barrel. If he smelled or tasted the fermented grape on her lips, he could punish her in the method that suited him best, perhaps even drowning her in wine!"[3]

Prohibiting drunkenness was a way to exert control over women's bodies. The strategy is quite literally ancient. In a poem called "Table Manners for Girls," the Roman poet Ovid writes that women ought not become intoxicated—or they deserve the consequence:

Pick food like fruit. It matters: eat with grace
And fingertips, not hands that grease your face.
And don't dine first at home; just stop before
You're full—at less than you can hold, not more;
If Paris had seen Helen eat with greed,
He'd have gone cold—"That mouth I do not need"—
And told himself that sort of snatch was stupid.
But girls may drink: Bacchus goes well with Cupid,

Provided you've a head, and you're not troubled
In feet or wit, and you don't see things doubled.
But lying drunk brings shame: if wine's untied them,
Girls deserve anyone who lies beside them.
Nor is it safe to sleep at the table: One
Easily does in sleep what is not done.[4]

H2O Vegetal

Each summer, natural winemakers hold a fair in southern Catalonia called H2O Vegetal. The fair is infamous for partying and drunken raucousness. My first year in Spain, I left the fair before night fell, but my second year, in 2019, I witnessed the bacchanal in full force. That year's iteration was held in El Pinell de Brai, a village in Terra Alta surrounded by mountains. In the morning, I got breakfast at a local bar with Carmen and Luis, who'd driven up from Torrijos, as well as an entourage of Catalan winemakers, including Manel Avinyó, known as "the Bubble Man" for his sparkling wines. We ate *a la Catalana*—heavy, with sausages and meats and wine—to prepare for the long day ahead, then walked over to the municipal gymnasium where the fair was held.

The gym was hot and crowded. I shouldered my way to winemakers' tables and thrust my glass through the mass of people, vying for a taste. There was talk of a pool somewhere in the gym complex; one man—a wine importer, I believe—encouraged everyone he met to take a naked swim that evening. I'd come with no plan, assuming I'd either find a ride back to Barcelona that afternoon or find a place to crash for the night. But as the day progressed, and as the crowd became looser, I realized very few people would be sober enough to drive me. Carmen and Luis left the fair as soon as the tasting portion ended, and two young Dutch winemakers who'd agreed to let me stay in their camper van left for dinner in another town.

My body was worn down from the hours of drinking. I could no longer feel the inside of my mouth. My gums were raw. My tongue and teeth were purple. Each new wine I drank seemed the same; I'd lost the ability to taste. A headache threatened from behind my temples, and my vision had begun to blur. The dull thrum of stress overtook my head and chest.

Outside, the night was dry and warm. Many winemakers had left the gym for their hotels, leaving behind stragglers who wanted to party with the day's dredges. Around me, people grabbed half-full bottles of wine and sloshed them into glasses. They spilled out into the parking lot, loitered around a bar. They swigged from bottles, stretched out on curbs, smoked cigarettes under the moonlight, laughing, their teeth stained red.

I had attended wine fairs before, and many of them progressed this way: professional tasting in the morning, partying at night. For the most part, the parties were light-hearted and joyous, with winemakers uncorking bottles of champagne and pouring free wine until the wee hours of the morning. Sometimes, though, I left these events feeling sick and raw. On the mornings after, I'd sludge through a hangover and wallow in self-disgust, ashamed at my participation in the hedonism of excessive drinking.

I struck up a conversation with a group of Italians gathered around the table for Cascina degli Ulivi, the winemaking estate of the late Stefano Bellotti. Considered the father of Italian natural wine, Bellotti died the previous fall, leaving behind a biodynamic farm in northwestern Italy's Piemonte. He started making wine in the late 1970s, when most Italian farmers were working large-scale and with chemicals, but his style of farming subverted those trends and promoted biodiversity. In the mid-2000s, he was denied European Union subsidies for planting fruit trees in the middle of his vines, which could no longer be legally considered a vineyard. Undeterred, he kept planting new crops, until harvest time of 2018, when he died of cancer.

His acolytes were friendly and knowledgeable, telling me of the vegetables growing around his property and giving me sips of his recent vintages—fresh and citrusy, or curiously spicy. Many were bronze or amber in color. These were orange wines, made of white grapes that spent time fermenting and aging on their skins, producing a darker color instead of the pale yellow that comes when grape skins are removed immediately from the juice before fermentation.

One of the Italians, a bespectacled physical therapist named Claudio, mentioned that he'd rented an Airbnb a few towns over. Sensing an opportunity, I told him I had no place to stay. His brow furrowed with concern, and he glanced around the gym. The air was stale. Someone had popped a bottle of champagne. "Stay on the couch," he told me, in Spanish. Perhaps this was risky, but he seemed kind—and, crucially, sober. I said yes.

The Italians and I left the fair's revelry and piled into a cab. At the house, we sprawled out on every surface—couches, armchairs, the floor. Claudio and I made plans to take a morning train back to Barcelona together, and, after wishing me goodnight, he went to his room. I curled up on the couch. Years later, I traveled to New York City to visit friends, and at a bustling pizza spot in Brooklyn, I spotted a Cascina degli Ulivi bottle on the wine menu. It was amber colored, made of white Cortese grapes harvested in 2010, when Bellotti was still alive, and, after we tasted, a friend said it smelled like violin rosin. For a moment, the wine launched me back in time, to the Italians who gave me a place to stay for the night. Even then, years later and thousands of miles away, I felt grateful.

Assault

A quiet place to sleep. How many times I had yearned for such a place. At age twenty-four, on a late-night bus to Brussels, the man sitting in the aisle seat next to mine stroked my thigh while I was trapped by the window. At age twenty-two, when I was reporting an article in Barcelona, a man at a bar pulled my dress up and thrust his hands under my tights, reaching into my underwear. When I was traveling alone in Europe at age eighteen, several years before meeting Carmen, men followed me down the street, pressed their lips to mine, pushed their hands up my skirt. One night in Lisbon, I blacked out from drinking. During a moment of hazy lucidity, I realized I was sitting alone at a dock, feet dangling over the Tagus River. I next remember tripping up stairs at my hostel, uncertain how I'd made my way back. I lost consciousness again. When I resurfaced, I was in my dorm, a man on top of me. Then, I was gone again. The next morning, I checked out of the hostel and walked to a pharmacy to purchase Plan B. I sat on a bench, blinking through harsh sunlight.

Soon after that night, a close friend died. She'd also been traveling in Europe for the same guide, and we talked nearly every day. Back on campus for my second year in college, I spent weekend nights alone in my bedroom, drinking whiskey straight from the bottle. I couldn't separate the grief for my friend from the grief for my body. I told myself it had been my fault, that I'd been too drunk, that I should have been more careful. There are many nights I cannot remember.

A Terrible Paradox

I never reported the man. At the time, I couldn't articulate how I felt, but I knew, intuitively, how the story would go. I was drunk and therefore an unreliable narrator of my own experience. My drinking would be to blame, not my perpetrator. Though I was only eighteen, I'd seen this play out enough on college campuses: rapists use alcohol as a tool to attack, and, when they are caught, as their go-to defense. I knew this, and yet, the other narrative—the rapist's narrative—shaped how I viewed my own rape. I blamed myself.

In the years that followed, I felt stuck in a terrible paradox. I surrendered my body to alcohol, as though preparing to re-enact the circumstance of my assault, as though trying to take back control. But in my attempt to regain control, I was losing it. My blackouts continued to the end of my final year in college, leading to weekends of exhaustion and lethargy. I was often sick, often unhappy, and sometimes I drank to distract from spiritual emptiness. Drinking became a way of self-negation. I wished I could simply disappear.

I had a problem, though I didn't fully admit it to myself until my drinking appeared to reach a climax one icy winter night. At a drunken celebration honoring the student newspaper's incoming editors, I gave a speech to a hundred of my peers while completely unconscious. I spent the next morning piecing together strange clues—ripped tights, heels abandoned in a friend's dorm—to understand what had happened. "Are you okay?" people asked when I saw them that day, the question caught somewhere between amusement and concern. I seized up in shame. All these people, many strangers, had an experience of my body to which I had not been witness. Only my searing hangover hinted at what I'd done to myself the night before.

God's Ladder

In Spain, I hoped that my drinking habits would become healthier. Vineyard work held the promise of making my body stronger. I wondered if seeing the process of winemaking, from pruning vines to stepping on grapes, could make me appreciate the drink more, respect it instead of abuse it. I wanted alcohol to be a joyful experience, as opposed to the experience of shame and hurt drinking had elicited during my years of avoidance and excess.

With Carmen and Barbara, drinking was study, meditation. We'd discuss the vineyard work, the vinification methods, how, exactly, the wine in my glass came to be. Discussions like these required a focus and thoughtfulness I'd never experienced while drinking, and I rarely got more than buzzed. Knowing where grapes were grown, I felt closer to the earth.

On their land, time slowed. I could lie on a warm boulder or listen to frogs for fifteen minutes and feel as though hours had passed. I would rest in the branches of a tall fig tree and watch the light change, or sit at the farmhouse window and watch starlings flit between the eaves. Nature demanded my attention. To sunsets. The blue after dusk. Peals of rain on the roof. Daylight filtered by a forest canopy. The sweep of wind through a field. Dewy grass. Swooping birds. Cold rivers. Mountains. Crickets. Clouds.

I recalled the oft-quoted Mary Oliver line, "Attention is the beginning of devotion." I saw this philosophy manifest in much of viticulture, past and present. In the Catalan region of Priorat, the monastery Cartoixa d'Escaladei, founded in the twelfth century by Carthusian monks from Provence, was a place where earthly and heavenly devotion came together. Escaladei is Catalan for "God's Ladder," and it was said that centuries ago, a shepherd had come to the place, in the foothills of the Monsant Mountains, and dreamt that angels there had descended from the heavens using a ladder propped against a pine tree. Today, the monastery is mostly in ruins; crumbling arches and columns remain.

Like other monks across Europe, the Carthusians at Escaladei had introduced viticulture to the region as a way to make sacramental wine and raise funds for the Catholic Church. In Catholic doctrine, wine was, and remains, a way to directly commune with God, a substance transformed into Christ's blood. The monks' lives were solitary, and cultivating vines was part of a daily rhythm that involved spiritual and secular tasks, from reading Biblical text to tilling soil. Such repetition itself was an act of prayer.

Court of Master Sommeliers

I'd wanted my story of wine to be one of transformation: from bad to good, from pain to pleasure—a neat binary. For a while, on the bucolic vineyards of rural Spain, that story was true. But as I moved deeper into the world of wine and learned more about the people who populated the industry, I reluctantly came to realize that wine could never be pure. The wine business, where drinking widely and frequently to expand one's palate is essential to career advancement, is steeped in quotidian violence. In fine dining, for example, workers are allowed very few bathroom breaks, if at all. One woman told me that when working in a fine dining restaurant, she bled through a $700 suit while on her period because she wasn't allowed to use the restroom. (Her bosses let her leave the restaurant early that day.) Another time that she was barred from the restroom, a urinary tract infection spread to her right kidney.

Another woman told me of her years working in New York City's wine industry, where, as a sommelier, she was subjected to a stricter dress code than her male colleagues. Patrons touched her legs as she poured bottles, and men spoke over her when she described the wines. Once when a wine distributor asked her on a date in exchange for a case of high-quality wine, her male supervisors told her she should go.

Both women had, at various times, been studying for certification from the Court of Master Sommeliers. Founded in England in 1977 as an international examining body, the Court offers prestigious certifications to sommeliers who pass its tests. In both Latin and middle French, the term sommelier's root words refer to a servant, one who might transport baggage for royalty, or care for pack animals that carried provisions on long trips.[5] The Court claims to build on this history of hospitality by improving beverage services in hotels and restaurants, and maintains that its mission is educational. Indeed, its members pride themselves on their vast accumulation of knowledge. Yet how, precisely, that knowledge should be attained—and what knowledge is worthy of having—is shrouded in secrecy. Various women told me that at the times they were studying, in the 2010s, the court provided little guidance on how to study for its examinations, nor did its examiners tell candidates who failed what they did wrong.

Earning the title of Master Sommelier is an arduous and nebulous process. First, candidates must progress through the "introductory," "certified," and "advanced" sommelier stages, each of which involves rigorous examinations. Obtaining the "master" title itself involves a multi-day exam testing the candidates on theory; proclivity for wine tasting; and service skills. Students must develop an encyclopedic knowledge of obscure wine facts—permitted grapes in Alsace Cremant wines, for example, or the river near which the Chinon wine appellation is located. They must also correctly identify the grape varieties, vintage, and region of three red and three white wines, down to the village and even specific tract of vines. To dedicate this much time and energy to wine, master sommelier Geoff Kruth says in the 2012 documentary *Somm*, "you have to be, just, you know, maybe a little bit off."[6]

Somm

Somm follows four master sommeliers, all men, as they study for the exam. The documentary portrays its protagonists as earnest, dedicated, and wildly intelligent, devoted to the pure pursuit of knowledge. They are obsessive and meticulous, their hunger for information geeky, yet cool. Sommeliers are, in the words of one chef interviewed in the film, the "rockstars of the restaurant industry."

One particular scene from the documentary captures the eccentricity of the exam and its students. About twenty minutes in, the four men sit around a wooden table, wine glasses lined in front of them. At the head of the table, Kruth, the master sommelier, speaks to the others like a football coach pumping up his players. "The wines," he says, using the language of conquest, "are there to be gotten." The others raise the glasses, swirl their contents, and lift them to their noses and mouths. As they sniff and taste, words spill from their lips in rapid succession. "Wine number one is a medium straw, kind of lemon yellow with golden green reflections moving into a watery meniscus" says one man, a former baseball player who, earlier in the film, was described by his wife as a "man's man." Another man says, "Nose is clean, uh, youthful. High intensity aromas. Maybe a little lanolin, wet wool, chalky limestone minerality."

After the men taste the wines, the camera cuts to a separate interview with Kruth. "Who makes great samurai swords?" he asks. "The person that's going to make a great samurai sword is the person who had a teacher who had a teacher, who had a teacher." On each repetition of the word teacher, the camera cuts to B-roll of different men: Kruth, then the master sommeliers Jay Fletcher and Fred Dame, the latter of whom co-founded the US chapter of the Court of Master Sommeliers. Until 2021, there was no study material or official curriculum for the exam, so students needed master sommeliers as teachers, teachers who would mentor them, and drink with them. Such teachers would bestow upon them the necessary knowledge to pass the exam, which could radically transform a sommelier's career, opening up opportunities to travel, earn higher salaries, and, in turn, teach others what they had learned.

As of 2022, there are one hundred and seventy-two possible teachers, and of those, twenty-eight are women. One hundred and forty-four are men.[7]

Blind Tasting

Like me, Madeleine Thompson had a story about wine that she had wanted to be true. After growing up in a chaotic household, learning about wine as a restaurant server had allowed her to connect with her otherwise preoccupied father, who worked as a wine steward in an Italian bistro and sold bottles at a liquor store. Wine made sense to her; it always had a *how* and a *why*. Wines tasted a certain way because they were made using specific grape varieties from particular places. "You can actually experience what you learn about,"

Thompson told me over the phone from Dallas, where she lives. "The sensory element of it is really intriguing."

In 2013, she sat for her level one Court of Master Sommelier examination. She passed. It was her twenty-first birthday. To celebrate, she went to a fine dining restaurant where she knew a master sommelier worked, hoping that he would offer his own wine pairings for her meal. When he came over to her table to talk, Thompson was "over the moon."

After dinner, the sommelier offered to hold a blind tasting for her in the apartment where she was staying. Thompson instead suggested they taste in a public space, but the restaurant they chose was closed so reluctantly, Thompson agreed to hold the tasting in her apartment. Inside, the sommelier told her to go to another room while he poured the bottles, so she wouldn't see their labels. When she returned, the sommelier had moved the wine glasses from the kitchen table to the couch. Uneasy, she began tasting the wines. Then, he forced himself on top of her. She pushed him off, horrified. "That was day one," Thompson told me.

She soon realized that her teachers were not all that interested in pedagogy. For them, knowledge was social capital that could be spent on ambitious young women grasping for ways to learn in an industry dominated by men. As Thompson tried to acquire the information she would need to pass her examinations—by attending conferences and competitions and wine trips abroad—she endured persistent sexual harassment and assault from the very people charged with mentoring her. A decade ago, a powerful sommelier wrote to her via Facebook that someone at an event had "asked me who the super hot chick in the second row was. I knew exactly who he was talking about." Fred Dame, the co-founder of the court's Americas chapter, called her "the prettiest little girl at TexSom," an annual wine industry conference held in Dallas.[8] Others messaged her on social media, or commented on her body. At one event, Thompson, the same powerful sommelier as before, and other wine professionals were gathered around a bar. The sommelier told Thompson he had a "special champagne" in his hotel room upstairs, and that he wanted her to try it. Instead of pouring her a glass, however, he grabbed her face and kissed her, and then forced himself on her. "I felt like I had to essentially give my body to wine," Thompson said.

The Banality of Men

Thompson is talkative and funny. Her conversations are peppered with both irony and sincerity, eloquence and swearing. On Facebook, her profile indicates that she is "in a relationship" with Champagne, and she warns followers that she mostly posts photos of her cats. Though her style is distinct, she speaks about wine like other women sommeliers I've met. Starting out in the business, they were drawn to wine's charm and artistry. And they were ambitious, imagining lives for themselves full of travel, intellect, delicious food. Yet they each quickly realized the industry, like every industry, is tainted with problematic power dynamics. Our circumstances were different, but I heard in their stories echoes of mine: their relationship with wine moved from idealization to deflation, from romance to reckoning.

In 2020, twenty-one women in the wine industry, including Thompson, recounted stories of sexual harassment and assault within the Court of Master Sommeliers to Julia Moskin at the *New York Times*. The accused included Dame, Kruth, and Devon Broglie, the president of the court's Americas chapter, none of whom responded to my requests for comment. These were stories of men propositioning them with promises of special wines. Of men offering to help improve their blind tasting skills. Of men getting drunk, or getting women drunk, and holding them hostage in hotel rooms. The men knew the power they wielded over students—the power to make a career, or to break it, should the women refuse their advances. Coercion, women told me, felt like an inevitability. And even if they were never propositioned, some people in the industry chalked women's successes up to the sexist, and usually false, presumption that they were having affairs with powerful men.

Sexual assault appears to be especially pervasive in the wine industry. Alcohol enables violence, the thinking often goes. I thought this myself when I subscribed to my family's views of alcohol and when I blamed drinking for making me vulnerable to assault. But, over time, I realized that *people* are those who give alcohol moral meaning. It's not intrinsic. The reality is far more banal, a story we are so accustomed to hearing. Men exploit power where they can find it—at a college party, a city street, a bar, a hostel. A wine tasting.

Nothing has Changed

Many people called for the accused men to be expelled from the Court of Master Sommeliers. Others demanded more transparency in the curriculum. Some called for the court to be dismantled entirely. Both Kruth and Broglie resigned.[9] In his resignation letter, Broglie, whose departure was, according to a court spokesman, "unrelated" to allegations of sexual impropriety, wrote, "I deeply apologize to all the women whose lives and careers have been negatively impacted by the predatory actions of any Master Sommelier. I put my best effort forward in changing the course of the organization, I recognize that my effort fell short." Kruth has, through his lawyer, denied any wrongdoing. In November 2021, the court moved to expel six of the 22 members it investigated. [10]

The organization updated its code of ethics, which members must sign in order to teach and examine candidates.

The code outlines the organization's general values (humility, integrity, hospitality, among others) and behaviors that might be at odds with those values.[11] They also established a hotline for candidates to report "treatment that is not fair and equitable."[12] (Emily Wines, who in the aftermath of the scandal took over as chair of the Americas chapter board of directors, wrote me that she couldn't comment on investigations, and declined to comment on how the court administered its examinations.)

But the women I spoke with see no reason to hope that the Court of Master Sommeliers will become safer. "Nothing has changed," Thompson told me, frustrated. Marie-Louise Friedland, a sommelier in Somerville, Massachusetts, said she was coerced into sex with her mentor while studying for the exam[13]. She told me that exclusivity "has been how they've always derived their power. Why would they ever let that go? It would diminish their standing in the industry. They truly believe that gatekeeping and knowledge hoarding is the best way to set a standard of education in the wine industry."

Some of the women have moved to new cities. Some have taken new jobs. Thompson no longer works as a floor sommelier; she now sells wine and spirits in Texas. In the years since the *New York Times* article was published, critics have harassed her on the internet and tried to get her fired from previous jobs. She's lost work, friendships. Customers still ask her on dates. She quit studying for sommelier exams long ago.

Quiet Rapture

A few summers back, I noticed my father sneaking sips of alcohol at unusual hours. I remembered his secret trips to the pizza parlor, his hidden beer. For the first time, I asked him about his drinking. By then, my relationship to alcohol had changed. I still drank, but not the way I did in college.

My father told me he was trying to quit. He'd been drinking for a long time as a way to cope with death and loss in his family. The Catholic Church, which his family attended, did not provide a spiritual home, and the nuns and priests in his schools were cruel. Later, when he had his own family, our version of Christianity was such that suffering belonged buried within oneself. Drinking dulled his pain. My mother, he told me, wanted to help him. I recognized that what I'd perceived as judgment was also a form of care.

I wanted to tell him my story, but I couldn't. Instead, over the phone one winter day, I told him I, too, had blacked out many times before. He paused, perhaps contemplating the significance of that statement. He told me he was sorry.

I'm not sure if my father believes in God. But every once in a while, I'll catch him in a state of quiet rapture. He'll become transfixed at lightning storms, snow-covered mountains—nature's graces. During a trip to the Olympic Peninsula in Washington State, he and I walked in a thicket of woods on a cape edged up against the Pacific. I went off down a trail without him, and when I returned, he pressed his cell phone toward me. He'd spent the previous half hour trying to capture the sound of waves crashing against the cliffs. Listen to this, he said, a staticky roar crescendoing from his phone.

FALL

Castilla-La Mancha, L'Albera, California

Vendimia

Late August was a time of waiting. Waiting to cut, waiting to press, waiting to make the wine we'd spent the year anticipating. All of the vineyard work led to this moment—winter and springtime pruning, spraying and fertilizing, tying and training branches. Carmen and Luis had spent the summer in parched Castilla-La Mancha watering the vines; Barbara and Carles had mended fences in an effort to fend off wild hogs. Both had monitored the dryness and heat with worry. If temperatures rose too much, grapes would stop growing.

I first returned to L'Albera for the white grape harvest. White grapes ripen faster than red grapes, so winemakers usually collect them earlier. The last time I'd seen the grapes, they were small and lime green. Now, they had ballooned to plump orbs of pale yellow and inky black. During the summer, I'd missed veraison, the onset of ripening, when the vines transition from energy production, through photosynthesis, to energy consumption, which gives size and color to the grapes.

As we waited for the perfect moment to cut, we were nervous. With her spraying and springtime pruning, Barbara had managed to fend off mildew. But she had another problem with the grapes. Ideally, acid and alcohol would complement each other, resulting in what winemakers call a "balanced" wine—higher acid with lower alcohol, and vice versa. This year, however, the state of grape ripening, which Barbara measured every few days, was precarious: the grapes' acidity was quickly dropping, but the potential alcohol content, measured in sugars, remained stubbornly low. Balance, therefore, was uncertain.

At daybreak, we collected a sample of grapes and mashed them into a pulp. Barbara smeared the juice onto a refractometer, a telescope-like instrument meant to measure sugar levels, and, putting the eyepiece to her face, frowned. She'd already tested for acid using a pH meter, and the two factors remained out of sync. "Shit," she groaned. She still wasn't sure—should we pick, or should we wait?

The Two Eighty Project

Four years after meeting Carmen and Barbara, I returned to California to work harvests. In Spain, I'd learned that generally, only people with upfront capital and access to land and cellar space can make wine a viable venture. Now, I realized this was especially true in California, where agricultural land is more expensive than most everywhere in the country.[1] In Europe, young winemakers often inherit land passed down over generations, continuing the tradition—and growing the wealth—of their ancestors. In California, by contrast, wine is a relatively new industry, and young, landless winemakers hoping to start their own businesses have to be creative. Many winemakers don't grow their own grapes and instead sign agreements to purchase fruit in bulk from larger and wealthier producers. Sometimes, they tend the vines in exchange for deals on purchasing the grapes. They rent cellar space and equipment—grape presses, stainless steel fermentation tanks, barrels, and pumps. The vineyards where they source their grapes are often hundreds of miles apart, requiring hours of driving during harvest season. Margins are so low that many small winemakers work other jobs—as bartenders, mostly, or, in the case of one woman I met, as a freelance fashion designer.

For all their romance, even the small family wineries where I volunteered in Spain were not immune to the pressures of capitalism. Two years after I met Carmen, her husband Luis lost his full-time job at his family's company when it went bankrupt. With a cellar full of bottles, the family feared they couldn't sell enough wine to keep up with the costs of operating their winery. One fall, they sold an entire tank of wine—some fifteen thousand liters—to a French company for cheap, just to make sure they'd sell at all. Barbara and

Carles, meanwhile, sometimes suffered crop loss as a result of volatile weather. To supplement their income, Barbara taught Italian at a local school, and Carles worked as a firefighter.

The barriers to entry for winemaking are high, and, as a consequence, the industry skews white and male. But Christopher Renfro, a thirty-nine-year-old Black winemaker in California, was trying to change that. We met in the fall of 2021, when I was spending a few months traveling around the San Francisco Bay Area to meet with winemakers, land owners, and vineyard workers. Renfro tended a tiny patch of vines in an unlikely place: a community farm on a hill overlooking Interstate-280, which cuts through the middle of San Francisco.

When I visited, the farm was lush, with bright red and orange tomatoes bursting from their tendrils and Mexican sage blooming deep purple. He didn't own the land—it was shared—but he dreamt of one day starting a venture on land in Louisiana that his family once possessed. His great-great-great-grandparents were enslaved, and when they were freed, they acquired land in the southern part of the state, where generations grew up and in turn raised their own children. But gradually, the family lost their land. Today, only six acres remain.

For Renfro, a former server and assistant wine director in a fine dining restaurant, farming and winemaking are acts of justice. He wanted to reclaim his family's land, promote Black land ownership, and bring the joys of gastronomy into communities typically excluded from fine dining. Through his work, including an initiative called The Two Eighty Project, a winemaking apprenticeship program for people of color, he hoped to bring people underrepresented in agriculture into fields like winemaking. Directly adjacent to his vines was a public housing community called Alemany Apartments, where more than a hundred families, many of them Black, lived. Yet, he said, few of them ever visited the farm. "There's project housing right there," Renfro told me. "It's a busy freeway. It's kind of weird that there's no grocery store, nothing in sight. It's an actual food desert next to a farm."

A few kids from the neighborhood helped Renfro plant new vines. They discussed the legacy of those vines and how they were shaping history with their own hands. Some vines, Chris told them, can live for a century. Come back in thirty years, he said, and see how they grow.

"A super expensive, stressful hobby"

Sonoma, California has ideal growing conditions for grapes. Summer nights are cold and misty, with the marine layer blowing east from the Pacific. Afternoons are hot and dry. This large diurnal shift—the difference between the nighttime low temperature and the daytime high—is good for the grapes, and allows ripening to slow and the pH to remain balanced. This results in a wine that tastes even, rather than overly alcoholic or acidic.

The fair weather can partially explain why land in Sonoma is so expensive. In 2021, vineyards sold for up to $215,000 per acre, and a typical single-family house in the area cost around $1.25 million, according to the real estate website Zillow.[2] In 2019, a ton of wine grapes grown in Sonoma and Marin counties sold, on average, for $2,845. By comparison, a ton in California's Central Valley, which grows more grapes than any other part of the state—and where poverty is generally higher than the state's average—sold for $301. (Most vineyards in Sonoma and the Central Valley are farmed conventionally, with pesticides.)

One September morning, I visited a harvest where I saw wealth and wage labor come together. The harvest took place at the home of a hobbyist winemaker, whose primary residence was in the Pacific Northwest. He bought his house, on what he calls one of Sonoma's "most exclusive" roads, a decade ago for about $400,000, and now he estimates the value is around $2 million. He, his wife, and two other couples shared the five-acre tract of vines, which backed up to their houses, and contracted other people to grow the grapes for them. Their vineyard manager, David Rothschild, was responsible for hiring workers, tending to the vines, and, ultimately, selling the grapes. Rothschild leased the site from property owners and took a cut of the grape sales with no cost for his services. But other property owners, Rothschild told me, forgo such deals and instead pay management companies $8,000 to $12,000 per acre in vineyard maintenance. "It's a super expensive, stressful hobby," Dan Marioni, one of Rothschild's business partners, said.

When I arrived at the vineyard around 8 a.m., the harvesters had already been working for three hours. They were picking grapes for various winemakers and were setting aside five hundred pounds for the property owner, who did not sell or make money off his wine. Usually, he kept it for home consumption, though he planned to bring bottles from the 2021 vintage to his upcoming business school reunion.

Wearing gloves, long-sleeved shirts, and hats, the workers proceeded quickly along the rows, clipping Syrah grapes and tossing them into plastic buckets that, when full, held forty pounds. Rothschild directed them in Spanish, telling them which rows to cut. As they worked, the property owner strolled though the vines, grinning. "This is beautiful," he said. He described to me a romantic vision of harvesters across the Northern Hemisphere picking grapes that very September day, as though he were taking part in something much bigger than his vineyard. "This is [also] going on in all these little villages in France."

Many of the workers came from Michoacán, Mexico, and some were undocumented. They earned around twenty-five dollars an hour during harvest, the most intense time of the year. One thirty-nine-year-old worker, Juan, first came to the United States when he was seventeen, and moved to California permanently fifteen years ago.

The rise of narco-trafficking had brought violence to his hometown, Juan told me, and he didn't have many work opportunities there anyway. After crossing the Sonoran Desert by foot, with a backpack full of water and cookies, he began working in Arizona's strawberry industry. Later, he moved to Santa Rosa, California, where he lived in one room with his wife and teenage son. At the time I met him, he worked multiple jobs—in grapes and in restaurants—to save money to bring his eleven-year-old son, who was still living in Michoacán, to California.

Some of the workers I met said they don't even drink the wine they helped make. For them, wine was work. For the property owner, wine was leisure. Their labor made possible his pleasure. Even though he outsourced all of his vineyard work, the property owner considered himself a farmer. Writing in a letter to his alumni magazine, he hoped that 2021 would be "the best vintage ever."

Wine Workers

The small Spanish wineries where I volunteered generally operated without employees, though during the two harvests I did with Carmen, she hired about a dozen day workers, usually local Moroccans, to pick grapes. Barbara and Carles, meanwhile, had Idreesa, the Gambian worker. Finding workers for the harvest is one of the most fraught aspects of operating a winery. During any given harvest,

Carmen employs friends, family, locals, and agriculture students looking for experience. For a few years, Carmen used a foreman to find her harvesters, but problems with paperwork and uncertainty over the workers' legal status led her to search elsewhere. During a recent harvest, Carmen hired college students who were back in their hometowns for the summer, and even more recently, she brought her oldest daughter, Andrea, into the winery as a paid contractor; she hopes the Spanish government will give Andrea a subsidy intended to attract young people to agriculture so Carmen can afford to hire her as a full-time employee. These fluid arrangements mean that each year, Carmen hires different workers for pruning and harvest. She spends much of her time teaching people how to cut vines, and consistency in vineyard work is impossible. "Everyone comes in with their own theory of how to do the work," Carmen told me.

As an employer, Carmen strictly follows government mandates, paying workers minimum wage, giving them ample break time, and providing plenty of water. She holds her harvests early in the morning, so workers don't have to pick in the heat of the day. And because she doesn't use pesticides, she protects their health. But this is not always the case. Around the world, agricultural workers, including grape pickers, are vulnerable to myriad abuses, from low wages to harsh working conditions.

In California, grape pickers often work in extreme heat and smoke, as harvest coincides with wildfire season. Law requires employers to give workers ten minute breaks every several hours, and even more breaks, termed "cool down rests," when temperatures exceed 95 degrees.[3] But enforcement is imperfect. In California's Central Valley, workers are often paid a piece rate, meaning they're paid per crate of grapes harvested, as opposed to an hourly wage, incentivizing pickers to work harder and faster.

In 2021, workers in Sonoma County protested for safer and more just working conditions.[4] Their protest is part of a long history of agricultural labor activism in California, largely driven by grape pickers. Indeed, the United Farmworkers emerged as a result of organizing around grape picking. In 1965, the Filipino labor group, called the Agricultural Workers Organizing Committee, decided to strike against table grape growers in Delano, California, to fight agricultural worker exploitation. The National Farmworkers Association, organized under Cesar Chavez, joined the cause a week later, and the next year, the two organizations merged, forming what is today the nation's largest farmworkers union.[5]

Among other demands, vineyard workers in Sonoma were fighting for compensation for lost wages when conditions—primarily wildfires—were too dangerous, and for hazard pay when they were required to show up for work. Wineries can obtain waivers that allow laborers to work in evacuation zones, even when everyone else is required to leave. Maria Salinas, a farmworker and organizer from Oaxaca, told Alleen Brown of *The Intercept* in the fall of 2021, "You're working and you're smelling the toxic smoke . . . And you don't want to protect yourself with the masks, because it's too hot, so you're breathing all of this. After work, you feel like sneezing and spitting. The saliva is black. If this is just what you're spitting, how must it be inside? What about your lungs?"

In Southern Europe, agricultural workers tend to immigrate from Morocco, Senegal, Gambia, and other parts of Africa, with some arriving on temporary work visas. Today, in southern Spain, many agricultural workers, documented and undocumented, live in shanty towns constructed of wood and plastic gleaned from the greenhouses where they work, year round, in freezing cold and sweltering heat.

In October 2021, Spanish police detained three people for luring migrant workers to the town of Valladolid during the grape harvest, and then "enslaving" them, according to *El País*. The workers harvested for little pay, if any, and slept on insect-infested mattresses in a ruined house in La Seca, known for its Verdejo wine.[6] In Champagne, France, managers of a company that provided agricultural services to winemakers were, in 2019, found guilty of human trafficking; they recruited hundreds of migrants to pick grapes, crammed them in unsanitary accommodations, and had them work 12 hours a day, often without pay.[7] Exploitation is rampant elsewhere around the world, from southern Italy to South Africa, especially in large-scale corporations that prioritize profit over everything else. And after the grape harvest, workers move on to the next: sugar beets, apples, olives, the products of their labor shipped across countries and seas, making their way to kitchens and tables.

Mari

When I was in California, a vineyard worker named Mari invited me to church with her on a Sunday. I'd met her at a Cabernet harvest in Sonoma and we immediately got along. Pensive and motherly, she described the life cycle of a grapevine while making tortillas on a portable stove during our break. As we sat eating in the cool morning, our fingers sticky with grape juice and slick from greasy grilled pork, she told me about the Catholic Church in Napa that Latino vineyard workers attend. Now, a few weeks later, she led me into its cavernous nave, and we took our seats on hard pews. A large wooden crucifix surrounded by long, illuminated glass rays hung at the altar. The glass at the top left of the crucifix was missing—shattered, Mari told me, during a recent earthquake. We folded our hands to pray.

Going to church with Mari showed me just one life behind the bottles I drink, giving a story to the often-faceless labor force responsible for bringing grapes from the vineyard into my glass. In her case, her job was a "blessing," Mari told me, in Spanish. She had stable employment at a small winery, a fair wage, and good working conditions. But she was an undocumented immigrant whose work status in the United

States was inevitably precarious. It took her years to land this kind of job at all.

Mari had lived in Napa for seventeen years. She moved there from Jiquilpan, a mid-sized town in Michoacán known for vibrant jacarandas that bloom violet every spring. In Jiquilpan, she dropped out of school at age thirteen and immediately went to work, first at a market selling sandwiches, and then at a tailor. At seventeen, she married, and a few years after that, she walked across the border into Arizona, following her husband to Napa, where he thought they'd be able to earn a better living.

Though she enjoyed Napa, Mari missed her hometown and her family. Those first years in California were lonely. She talked to her mother on the phone every day and invested in the church community as a way to "fill the hole in my heart." In April of 2017, she started a job at a small family winery in Sonoma, thanks to a connection from her brother, who had already been working in local vineyards. She was initially wary. "Sometimes I'd see workers in the fields and think, 'oh, poor them, it's too hot,' or 'it's too cold,'" Mari told me. "I didn't feel capable." But soon, she fell in love with vineyard work. She learned quickly.

Shortly after she started working at the winery, Mari received terrible news. Her mother had gone walking in the Jiquilpan countryside and never returned. "It's something you can't explain," Mari told me. "You're in country so far away, and your mother has gone missing, and you can't do anything." The family searched for two weeks, and she was eventually found, dead. Mari believes her mother had overexerted herself and died in the night.

Because she is undocumented, Mari couldn't go home for her mother's funeral lest she risk being denied re-entry to the United States. She hasn't, in fact, been back to Jiquilpan since she left all those years earlier. Distraught, she turned to the vineyard for solace. The work kept her mind off her mother, kept her focused on creating something. "The vineyard was my best therapy," Mari said. "What a marvel, nature. From the moment you prune. The sprouts emerge, then the leaves." Her favorite time of year was harvest. She loved it for the same reasons that I love the harvest, and that Carmen and Barbara love the harvest. Mari liked the feeling of completion—a year's worth of labor finished once the grapes are cut from the vine.

After church, Mari invited me to her house for lunch. First, we stopped at La Morenita, a boisterous market filled with meats and spicy candies. Mari bought Oaxacan cheese and cream, and we drove another few minutes into a quiet neighborhood. In her sunlit kitchen, Mari pulled out a tortilla press a friend had brought her from Mexico, flattened homemade dough, and lowered the tortilla into a pan of hissing oil. She drizzled the fried tortilla with cheese, cream, salsa verde, and lettuce, and opened a wine for us to try. It was Chardonnay, co-fermented with peaches she'd helped pick from the winery's fruit trees.

Mari likes harvesting Chardonnay. It's a large grape, collected later in the season than other white varieties, which means it's usually hot out for the harvest; a few weeks earlier, she'd collected Chardonnay at 3 a.m., under the light of large lamps. It rained during another recent day collecting grapes, soaking her body the whole day—a beautiful respite from California's endless drought, she said, smiling. Mari used to harvest with her brother alongside her, but the previous winter, immigration officials stopped him at the border and prevented him from entering the country. Now, he's in Mexico, biding his time until he can return.

Sometimes people ask Mari what she'd do first if she was able to return to Jiquilpan. Once, her husband answered for her: She'd visit her siblings. "No," Mari corrected him. "I would go see my mother's tomb."

Smoke Tainted

Until recently, I didn't know California wine at all; I moved out of state at seventeen, too young to visit wineries. But I wondered if I would find some glimmer of recognition, some memory from my childhood articulated in the flavor of a wine made in the hot and dry conditions of my home state. Growing up near Southern California's desert, I spent the first week of each school year sweating in the August heat. In October 2007, the Witch Creek Fire in San Diego, whose suffocating smoke traveled forty miles north to Temecula, shuttered schools for a few days. In the intervening decade, fires have become more destructive and more frequent. In

2020, the August Complex Fire alone burned more than a million acres on the northern California coast, making it the largest in state history.[8]

I'd heard of smoke-tainted wines, made from grapes whose skins absorbed noxious burn fumes. What, I wondered, does a wildfire taste like?

One afternoon, I traveled to Napa Valley for a tasting with my brother. In some places on the drive, the landscape looked familiar—parched, dusty, brittle. I watched as the golden hills unfurled beside me. Some looked smeared with charcoal, marking the destructive path of wildfires from years past. A road sign asked, "Ready for wildfire? What's your escape route?"

When I stepped out of the car, a wave of dry heat washed over my face, as though I'd opened an oven. The air smelled of sage and chaparral, of kindling. The year before, wildfires had ravaged Napa Valley's eastern hills, burning several wineries to the ground. The quantity of grapes pressed for wine was down 40 percent due to fires, the state's drought, and smoke, which had damaged many surviving grapes.[9]

Like cigarette smoke embedded in motel-room carpets, wildfire smoke is nearly impossible to extract from wine. Smoke molecules bind with sugar, the compound that makes fermentation possible, meaning that once smoke permeates grape skin, it's there to stay.[10] The worst-hit wines were the valley's famed—and expensive—Cabernets, those late-maturing, heavy reds whose harvest falls during peak wildfire season. Smoke-tainted wines are usually reds, because they often involve extended time steeping with skins. Many winemakers decided to forgo bottling Cabernets at all, worried smoke taint would tarnish their reputations.

At the tasting, I asked to try wildfire wine, and to my surprise the sommelier poured a white variety (a Riesling) that was infected with smoke. The winery had tried to mask the smoke by permitting the wine to undergo malolactic fermentation, uncommon for the variety. The Rieslings I had tried during my time in Europe were light and fruity, but this one was muted, smelling faintly of tobacco. I raised the glass to my lips and frowned, imagining infernal, orange skies. One winemaker told me smoke-tainted wine tasted like an ashtray. Another said it was like the steam from water used to put out a campfire. Embers, cigarettes, barbecue—I'd heard all these words before. "I feel the smoke taint more than I taste it," my brother said, and I agreed. It was like a subtle burn at the back of the throat, a burn that lingers.

Exceptional Drought

Drought wines have another taste altogether. They are alcoholic and rich. Strained for water, vines produce fewer grapes than normal, and, in turn, sugars are concentrated in those grapes, making the wine heavier and more intense in flavor. Vines are hardy plants, generally well-adapted to water scarcity. But extreme lack, and extreme heat, can stunt grape growth.

The part of California where I grew up has been spared the fires; nothing I love there has burned. But droughts are becoming more persistent. When I was a child, yard signs that said "brown is the new green" encouraged residents to turn off their sprinklers to conserve water. I ran with the track team in ninety-degree weather and once fainted during a soccer game on a scorching afternoon. During a heatwave in 2018, one of my mother's chickens fell ill in its coop, then died. Temperatures are regularly in the triple digits. Rainfall is cause for celebration.

According to the US Drought Monitor, 47 percent of the state—including Napa and Sonoma counties—suffered "exceptional drought," the most severe of its categories, in the late summer of 2021.[11] That August, Central Valley water authorities banned farmers from using rivers for irrigation.[12] For the first time ever, the state shut down Lake Oroville's hydroelectric plant, warning that the water levels would soon be insufficient to generate power.[13] Hundreds of thousands of salmon died in the Klamath River, where increased water temperatures allowed parasites to flourish.[14]

The US Drought Monitor compiled the most apocalyptic effects into a bullet point list:[15]

- Fields are left fallow

- Orchards are removed

- Vegetable yields are low

- Honey harvest is small

- Fish rescue and relocation begins

- Pine beetle infestation occurs

- Forest mortality is high

- Wetlands dry up

- Survival of native plants and animals is low

- Fewer wildflowers bloom

- Wildlife death is widespread

- Algae blooms appear

Other effects, not listed, include: Weakened vines, endangering future crops. Inhibited photosynthesis, and, in turn, unripe grapes. Harvest, once a time of joy, becomes a time of unease. One wildfire, one hot spell, could wipe out years' worth of labor. When there is no water, there are no grapes.

Wines of a Changing World

In August 2021, the sky was dim. The fog rolling in from the San Francisco Bay didn't break; by midday, it warped into a stagnant haze. I gravitated toward water to recall its abundance, and to escape the heat. I sought out redwoods, picturing water coursing up their massive trunks from the soil deep beneath my feet.

It was only the beginning of wildfire season and already I had lost track. Was this smoke from the Dixie Fire? The Antelope Fire? Wildfires, I learned, get their names from the places they originated. Country roads. Rural towns. Mountain peaks. I wondered what the next one would be christened.

Watching the inferno sky take shape, I realized harvest was underway in some parts of the state. In other areas, winemakers were anxiously waiting to pick. Some had tried to prepare for the unavoidable. They grafted vines onto drought-resistant rootstocks. They pruned vines so that leaves could eventually shade grapes from sunburn, or they removed leaves so that grapes might ripen faster for earlier picking. They picked earlier anyway—making wine that was more acidic and less alcoholic—to avoid harvesting during the worst wildfire months, September and October.

When winemakers inevitably evacuate, they leave their grapes hanging on the vine to collect ash or burn; they abandon their juice in the cellar as it's fermenting. If the wildfires don't directly torch their vineyards, winemakers adapt. They use temperature controls in fermenting tanks to separate grape juice from ash. They make rosés instead of reds, removing smoky skins before the taste of wildfire overwhelms.

Around the world, climate change is altering wines. Where it was once too cold to grow vines, farmers are now finding warmer temperatures suitable for viticulture. Elsewhere, the changes are devastating. Unseasonable hail and frost have destroyed crops in France.[16] Germany's vineyards were washed out during floods in the summer of 2021.[17] In warmer regions, like Carmen's, alcohol content is creeping up. Those wines taste like a heating planet.

When the world is on fire, wine may not seem a particularly grievous loss. But if, recalling Carmen's words, wines are a historical record—of the land, the climate, the people who make it—they are also memory keepers, reminding us of a time when the earth was able to produce such flavors. The wines of the past are long gone.

"I'm starting to get worried," Barbara told me one particularly hot afternoon, several years after I lived with her in L'Albera. In 2020, she lost ninety percent of her grapes to drought. In July of 2022, she was already seeing burned leaves, and the grapes were smaller than usual. "It's not just the drought, it's physically, as I age, being able to endure this kind of heat. I don't see the future." The Spanish and Catalan governments, she told me, didn't give aid for grapes lost to heat or cold—only a small amount for mildew damage. "It's not enough," she said.

In August of 2021, I drove to Treasure Island in the San Francisco Bay to help a friend bottle his 2020 wines. That year, he told me, was "pretty miserable." Lightning storms struck Santa Cruz and Mendocino counties, where he grows grapes, resulting in the massive August Complex Fire. Ash covered his vineyards, and smoke during harvest made breathing difficult. With his red grape varieties, he decided to make rosés to avoid the worst effects of smoke taint. "Pink wines," he said, shaking his head. He was bored of them, but as long as wildfire smoke choked up his harvests, stronger red wines were not viable.

When we finished work for the day, my friend gifted me a few bottles from 2020. I thought about saving them for a while, to recall the time and place from which they came, that year of fire and storms and heat. But they were young wines, made without barrel aging, and best to drink when they're fresh. On an evening about a month after harvest, I opened a bottle to share with friends. It was cool and light, quenching my thirst.

Pigéage

Eventually, grapes must be cut. In 2018, in L'Albera, after a few days of wavering, Barbara and Carles made the decision to harvest their Garnacha Blanca. The afternoon before we cut, the sky was dark. A heavy rain fell. I opened the window and felt the softness in the air that comes with the Tramuntana. The land, I worried, would be too muddy for us to walk up and down the rows. The rain would dilute grapes. The potential alcohol content would never rise. But when I raised my concerns to Barbara, she glanced up from her cup of tea. "This is nothing," she said. "We're working tomorrow."

Coordinating harvest is a balancing act. Barbara had been on the phone all day, calling friends to ask if they'd help pick. Often, winemakers don't make a decision to cut until the night before, and few people can drop everything on a moment's notice to harvest unless they're seasonal workers used to the rhythms of viticulture. For winemakers who don't own equipment, arranging rentals for transport and grape presses can prove complex, especially for those whose vineyards and cellars are far apart (refrigerated trucks are essential, lest the grapes start to ferment on long, hot drives). Cellar space becomes an issue as well; winemakers must clear out the previous year's vintage from their tanks in order to make room for incoming grapes.

The work was, of course, work—hours of hard labor in service to another person's business—but at times it felt idyllic, especially during Barbara's harvest. There were fifteen or twenty of us, all friends who'd come to volunteer our time and bodies in exchange for meals and wine. There were volunteers who'd come from Banyuls in southern France; a teacher from Barcelona; a British gardener living in Terra Alta. Over the course of a week, we cut Tempranillo and Cariñena, red and white Garnacha, bunches of grapes piling up in heavy crates. Each day after we finished working, Barbara made pasta or pizza, and we'd drink and talk until nightfall. Once when there was a lull between work days, I gathered blackberries from the riverbank and baked a cobbler.

Trucks hauling grapes rattled up and down dirt roads: Everyone in town was harvesting. Months before, a winemaker had advised me to look at people's hands during the harvest. "You know everything about them," he'd told me. Now, I saw farmers whose fingers were stained with red grape juice. I saw hands hardened and latticed with cuts from years clutching shovels, cutting branches, driving tractors.

After a few days, Barbara's eyes were tired. There was more work to be done, thousands of pounds of grapes to be cut between dawn and midday, thousands to be pressed and bled and poured into vats. If the yeasts were healthy and the temperature was just right, the juice would begin to move by its own accord, churning and fermenting.

In order to produce something drinkable, winemakers carefully monitor the fermenting juice and determine when to intervene to create the style and flavor of wine they desire. (If crushed grapes are left in a bucket for a week, they'll probably ferment, but the result will likely be disgusting.) As the fermenting juice releases carbon dioxide, the solid elements, include grape skins and stems, rise to the top, creating a layer called a cap. Because the solids are high in tannins, winemakers often mix them back with the liquid to create a richer wine and avoid bacterial buildup. To do so, they might perform pumpovers—pumping juice from the bottom to the top of a tank and splashing it over the cap—or punch-downs, which involve stomping on the cap or pushing the material back down to the bottom with a tool that looks like a massive potato masher.

Sometimes, winemakers suffer what is known as a stuck ferment, which happens when yeasts aren't catalyzed to consume the sugars. To solve this problem, winemakers often press smaller amounts of grapes by foot, a process known in French as "pigéage à pied," in the hopes that the yeast from micro-batch fermentation will kickstart fermentation at the larger scale.

Carles and Barbara didn't have a stuck ferment, but they wanted me to stomp on grapes anyway. Those grapes had gone through a carbonic maceration: when whole grapes ferment in tanks with ample carbon dioxide, and then are crushed. I objected—I'd sliced open a toe on a cinderblock the week prior—but gave in. "Fermentation kills everything," Carles told me, grinning, as I lowered myself into the tub of fruit, sugary juice stinging my small wound.

Thousands of Pounds

A week after harvesting in L'Albera, I traveled south, back to Castilla-La Mancha. It was sweltering out, but Carmen insisted we wear long sleeves and pants to protect our skin from the intense sun. "It's what the professionals do," she told us. During four days of harvesting, we collected 88,000 pounds of grapes, and I felt the massive numbers in my arms, legs, back. After each day, a refrigerated cargo truck drove the grapes twenty-five miles east, to the cellar, and a handful of workers spent half an hour throwing thirty-pound boxes of grapes into a de-stemming machine. The de-stemming machine partially crushed the grapes, and Carmen and Luis then pumped that liquid, with the skins, into tanks. After a week, we pressed the grape skins to squeeze the last amount of juice out of them (for greater complexity in the wine) and then removed the wine from its skins. The work was messy, and we spent much of our time in the cellar cleaning spills. With Carmen, I stood inside the tank, knee-high in steamy grape skins, and scraped the grapes out of the tank with a pitchfork. "Castilla La-Mancha me mancha," I joked to Carmen, my voice echoing in the stainless steel vessel. *Castilla La-Mancha stains me!* By the end of each day, my hands were the color of maraschino cherries. The stain took weeks to fade.

Fermenting wine secretes massive amounts carbon dioxide. Before each day of cellar work, Carmen advised me to wait outside as she and Luis opened windows and doors to aerate the space. She told me of a young winemaker from Galicia who was taking samples from the fermenting wine when she inhaled too much carbon dioxide. She fell into the fermenting grape juice, and her body was found in the vat the next day.

We waited for the grape juice to begin fermenting. When it did, usually a few days after harvesting the grapes, we mixed the fermenting liquid so the skins didn't dry out. Using a tube called a hydrometer, Carmen measured the density of the juice to determine when fermentation had finished.

One evening between harvest days, Carmen, Luis and I returned to the vineyard to sample one section of the Graciano parcel for the grapes' sugar and acidity levels. While they went off to check on a broken hose, I climbed into a fig tree. I plucked a piece of fruit from the branches, the fig's soft skin tearing easily into sweet, pulpy flesh. Dusk hung over the land. The setting was muted except for the occasional distant dog bark and car horn. I stretched back and felt the soreness in my body, from the days of cutting, lifting, and scraping.

During my time in Spain, I often found myself overwhelmed. There were so many languages to study, places to visit, people to meet. Even the world of wine, a small subculture, felt impossibly large, impossible to know in its entirety. After a year in the country, I wasn't sure what I'd do with everything I had learned. But, registering the quiet ache in my arms and legs while resting in the branches, I felt the satisfaction of a good day's work. That was enough.

Making Wine with a Woman

On the second morning of harvest, we were up before the sun, rubbing sleep from our eyes as the car sped to the vineyard in Santa Olalla. The morning sky changed from black to deep blue to a soft violet, then pink, and I gazed out the window, watching the gentle hills spread out before us in all directions. In the vineyard, we were surrounded by a sea of leafy grape vines. A star faded in the sky. Carmen handed out gloves and shears.

"Listen," Carmen said to the group of workers gathered around her. There were sixteen of us: Carmen's children, friends, and contract workers from around the region. "Don't cut anything dehydrated, or any of the small bunches high up. And no leaves. Please, no leaves."

We inched along the rows of grape vines. Our hands were machines clutching deep purple bunches, searching for the stem, slicing the grapes from the vine, tossing the grapes into crates. A tractor whirred. Harvesters traded jokes. Shears chopped and cracked wood. Every once in a while, I looked up to watch the men work. Sometimes they cut unripe bunches, or forgot ripe grapes, or cut too close to the vines, vines that we had spent those long February days working to shape. Their carelessness pained me. I wanted to yell out across the vines, to warn them that their negligence could permanently damage the plants. But I kept my concerns to myself. I watched Carmen watching them, her sharp eyes missing nothing.

The sun blazed on the back of my neck, and my shirt dampened with perspiration. It was 85 degrees out with no wind. By the end of the day, we had collected 20,000 pounds of grapes. My arms were limp, my back sore.

After we finished, I peeled my gloves from my clammy hands. A man, his face shaded by a wide-brimmed straw hat, approached me, twirling his shears. "You're the American, right? What do you think of this work?"

I liked it, I told him. "It's really hard, but I'm happy to do it. I'm learning so much."

"You girls work slower than everyone else," he said. "The guys are just faster, but that's okay, that's normal. You girls are thorough."

I glanced at Carmen, wondering if she'd heard. She was standing a few meters away examining a row of vines.

Carmen frowned, picked a bunch of grapes from the vine, and held them up. "Come over here," she yelled to the man next to me. "Your guys missed all of these grapes." He opened his mouth to yell back, but said nothing and trudged over with three men to finish collecting what they'd missed.

Carmen supervised the men as they worked, correcting their mistakes. As she walked down the row, some of the grape vines reached her neck. A few towered over her head. I hardly noticed, because in that moment she seemed taller than everything, taller than the grape vines and olive trees and the telephone wires in the distance. Taller than the men, too.

EPILOGUE

Graciano, 2018

Four years after picking grapes in Castilla-La Mancha, I found Carmen's wine at a bar in Las Vegas, where I now live. I'd left Europe, and because of the Covid-19 pandemic, I hadn't been able to see Carmen for two years, though we exchanged messages from time to time. She shared updates on the grapevines and her family, and I recounted cross-country road trips.

Friends and family were bemused when I moved to Las Vegas from northern California, leaving obvious abundance for the desert. But working with vines inspired a curiosity about the world around me, and now, the land itself was teaching me to look closer. Whereas I once may have viewed Las Vegas as a desolate collection of strip malls and casinos, today I see a city sprawled across an ancient, living crust of rock, algae, and lichen. I see a valley formed by sandstone mountains, with ridges covered in junipers and pinyons, and cholla and creosote growing at lower elevation. I even see my childhood home, a place I'd once defined only by what it lacked, in a new light. Temecula is full of astonishing life—chaparral shrubs and orange trees, buckwheat and white sage. A gap in the mountains, I've realized belatedly, carries in fog from the ocean, accounting for cold nights even in the scorching summer. And yes, there are seasons—subtler than those in other places, but quiet shifts that move plants and animals through their annual rhythms nonetheless.

At the Las Vegas bar, the wine I found was made of a single variety, Graciano, from the year I'd harvested with Carmen. Her wine is difficult to find in the United States, and I was amazed I found this particular bottle, surely one of the few remaining from that vintage, in such an unlikely place, a world away from the plains of central Spain. When I bought the bottle, the bartender told me it was the last they had in stock.

The next night, I poured it for my partner to try. We were on my bed, the only place to sit in my tiny downtown apartment, and the window was open. The wind rattled my blinds, drifting in with sounds of the street—ambulances, arguments. We examined the wine's color, like Carmen had taught me; it was deep red in the fading light. He brought glass to his nose. "It smells like a forest floor," he said. I laughed; a friend had told me the same thing a few years earlier. Both men grew up surrounded by woods, so the smell was familiar: humid, musty, pungent like decaying leaves.

I breathed deep. The year of labor came back to me—gray mornings pruning vines, long hot days cutting grapes during harvest. Perhaps I'd touched that very bottle; I'd helped Carmen with cellar work throughout 2019, bottling and labeling and packing up wine to ship elsewhere. To me, the wine smelled like those early days in Spain, like the tastings Carmen gave at the roadside bar in Castilla-La Mancha with her friends. I remembered the fermented garlic, the hours-long sobremesas, my struggle to speak. I remembered how the wine smelled, to Carmen, like chicken blood, a memory from her own childhood. Our memories were now merging, mine building on hers, becoming something new. I poured another glass.

ACKNOWLEDGEMENTS

I started writing this book during a cold winter in Somerville, Massachusetts, and ended during the balmy early autumn of Las Vegas, with stints in Asheville, Temecula, and Oakland in between. During those nearly two years, many people supported me as I worked on the manuscript. Thank you, firstly, to Haaris, Chris, and Ian for bringing this project to life. Thank you to the brilliant and generous Tajja Isen for pushing me to write early versions of some of this work through a delightful column in *Catapult*. Earlier than that, Rachel Signer assigned several pieces for her lovely indie wine publication *Pipette*, and through that work and her editing, I learned how to write about wine. I wrote my first-ever piece about wine for *Guernica* in 2018, and am grateful to Jennifer Gersten for assigning it. Alice Feiring plucked my essay out of a slush pile for her 2019 wine writing contest, and since then I've been fortunate to benefit from her gracious mentorship and encyclopedic knowledge of the wine world. Other parts of this book began as essays with the *Virginia Quarterly Review* and *Off Assignment*; thanks to Paul Reyes, Heidi Siegrist, and Sophie Haigney.

Many people read early versions of this work. Thank you to Alex Erdekian, Haley Baker, Benjamin Sher, Amelia Nierenberg, Julia Fine, Grace Mitchell Tada, Colleen Murphy, Humberto Juarez Rocha, Abbygale Musgrove, Oona Robertson, Krista Diamond, and Rachel Walker. Particular thanks to my genius pal Maia Silber for helping me clarify my own thinking, and to Michael Rudolph, who gave me more comments (all wonderful!) on the book than any other person. Thanks to Kimon de Greef and Sarah Trent, too, for support. I am grateful to all the people who put up with me when we drink wine together, most frequently: Clement Gelly, Ellen Schmidt, Bridget Bennett, Trisha Thadani, Reis Thebault, Vivian Wang, Miguel Otárola, Tim Tai, Julia Cohn, Jonah Hahn, Julia Argy, Amy Weiss-Meyer, Nick Fandos, and Jamie Lee Solimano. Special thanks to Molly and Drew. For general life support, thanks to both of them, and to Mom, Dad, and Grandma.

Winemakers, growers, pickers, and restaurant workers, some of whom are named in the book and others who are not, are the heart of this work. Thank you to all of them, especially Carmen and Barbara, for teaching me everything.

NOTES

Preface

1 Evans-Pritchard, E. E. "Nuer Time-Reckoning." *Africa*, vol. 12, no. 2, 1939, pp. 189–216., https://doi.org/10.2307/1155085.

Chapter 1

1 Trenda, Eloise. "Wine Production Volume in Spain by Region." *Statista*, 8 Feb. 2022, https://www.statista.com/statistics/463936/production-volume-of-wine-in-spain-by-region/.

2 Robinson, Jancis. "Castilla-La Mancha." *Castilla-La Mancha | JancisRobinson.com*, https://www.jancisrobinson.com/learn/wine-regions/spain/castilla-la-mancha.

3 Farmer, Erica A. "Codifying Consensus and Constructing Boundaries: Setting the Limits of *Appellation D'origine Contrôlée* Protection in Bordeaux, France." *PoLAR: Political and Legal Anthropology Review*, vol. 37, no. 1, 2014, pp. 126–144., https://doi.org/10.1111/plar.12054.

4 "Appellation D'origine Controlée (AOC)." *Champagne.fr*, https://www.champagne.fr/en/terroir-appellation/appellation/appellation-origine-controlee-aoc.

5   Agencia Estatal de Meteorologia. "El Año 2017 Fue El Más
    Cálido y El Segundo Más Seco En España Desde 1965 ."
    AEMET, Spain, 10 Jan. 2018, http://www.aemet.es/en/noticias
    /2018/01/Resumen_climatico_2017.

6   Leitao, David D. "The Thigh Birth of Dionysus: Exploring
    Legitimacy in the Classical City-State." *The Pregnant Male as
    Myth and Metaphor in Classical Greek Literature*, Cambridge
    University Press, New York City. 2014, pp 58-99.

7   Britannica, The Editors of Encyclopaedia. "Orphic
    religion." *Encyclopedia Britannica*, 10 Jun. 2008, https://www
    .britannica.com/topic/Orphic-religion.

8   Pliny the Elder, Natural History, BOOK XVII. "The Natural
    History of the Cultivated Trees. Chap 3. What soils are to be
    Considered the Best." http://www.perseus.tufts.edu/hopper/
    text?doc=urn:cts:latinLit:phi0978.phi001.perseus-eng1:17.3

9   Williams, Gavin. "Slaves, Workers, and Wine: The 'Dop
    System' in the History of the Cape Wine Industry, 1658–
    1894." *Journal of Southern African Studies*, vol. 42, no. 5,
    2016, pp. 893–909, https://doi.org/10.1080/03057070.2016
    .1234120.

10 Mejia, Paula. "The Gnarled History of Los Angeles's
    Vineyards." *Atlas Obscura*, 3 July 2018, https://www
    .atlasobscura.com/articles/history-of-california-wine.

11 Thomas Pinney. "Chapter 8, Eastern Viticulture Comes of
    Age: The Grape Boom in the Old South." *A History of Wine
    in America*, UC Press E-Books Collection, 1989, https://
    publishing.cdlib.org/ucpressebooks/view?docId=ft967nb63q
    &chunk.id=d0e6202&toc.id=d0e5748&toc.depth=1&brand
    =ucpress&anchor.id=bkd0e6311#X.

12 Smith, Christian. "Five of the Most Expensive Bottles of Wine
    in the World." *The Drinks Business*, 10 Mar. 2022, https://www

.thedrinksbusiness.com/2022/03/five-of-the-most-expensive
-bottles-of-wine-in-the-world/.

13 "Domaine De La Romane-Conti," http://m.romanee-conti.fr/
familles.php.

14 See Domaine De La Romane-Conti website, https://www
.romanee-conti.fr/

15 Pomranz, Mike. "This Is the World's Most Expensive Bottle
of Wine." *Food & Wine*, Food & Wine, 16 Oct. 2018, https://
www.foodandwine.com/news/most-expensive-wine-auction
-romanee-conti-burgundy.

16 "Discover Ann Noble's Aroma Wheel." *Discover Ann Noble's
Aroma Wheel*, https://www.winearomawheel.com/ann-noble
-aroma-wheel.html.

17 See WSET website, https://www.wsetglobal.com/about-us/
what-we-do/

18 McCoy, Elin. *The Emperor of Wine: The Remarkable Story of
the Rise and Reign of Robert Parker*, Grub Street, London,
2008, p. 98.

19 Mobley, Esther. "Wine's Diversity Issue Starts with the Way
We Talk about the Taste of Wine." *San Francisco Chronicle*, 8
Sept. 2020, https://www.sfchronicle.com/wine/article/Wine-s
-diversity-issue-starts-with-the-way-we-15544232.php.

20 de Leon, Miguel. "It's Time to Decolonize Wine." *PUNCH*,
26 June 2020, https://punchdrink.com/articles/time-to
-decolonize-wine-sommelier-racism-restaurants/.

21 Northwestern University. "Why Odors Trigger Powerful
Memories." *Medical Xpress - Medical Research Advances
and Health News*, Medical Xpress, 8 Mar. 2021, https://
medicalxpress.com/news/2021-03-odors-trigger-powerful
-memories.html.

Chapter 2

1   *The Soils | Do Empordà.* https://www.doemporda.cat/en/the
    -soils.html.

2   Burns, Scott. "The Importance of Soil and Geology in Tasting
    Terroir with a Case History from the Willamette Valley,
    Oregon." *The Geography of Wine*, 2011, pp. 95–108., https://
    doi.org/10.1007/978-94-007-0464-0_6.

3   Ibid.

4   O'Keefe, Kerin. "The Volcanic Wines of Italy." *Wine
    Enthusiast*, 16 Jan. 2018, https://www.winemag.com/2018/01
    /16/volcanic-wines-italy/.

5   White, Robert. *Understanding Vineyard Soils*, Oxford
    University Press, New York City, 2009, p. 8.

6   Burns,"The Importance of Soil and Geology in Tasting Terroir
    with a Case History from the Willamette Valley, Oregon."

7   Reverte, Jorge Martínez. *La Batalla Del Ebro*. Planeta
    DeAgostini, Barcelona, 2005.

8   "Grand Cru Classes EN 1855." *Site Officiel Bordeaux.com*,
    https://www.bordeaux.com/gb/Our-Terroir/Classifications/
    Grand-Cru-Classes-en-1855.

9   Wilson, Jason. "Dangerous Grapes." *Godforsaken Grapes:
    A Slightly Tipsy Journey through the World of Strange,
    Obscure, and Underappreciated Wine*, Abrams Books, 2018, p. 15.

10 Matasar, Ann B. "Women Need Not Apply." *Women of Wine:
    The Rise of Women in the Global Wine Industry*, University of
    California Press, Berkeley, 2006, p. 10.

11 "What Is Biodynamics?" *What Is Biodynamics? | Biodynamic
    Association*, https://www.biodynamics.com/what-is
    -biodynamics.

12 Church, Ruth Ellen. "Do Wines Make Women Giggly?" *Chicago Tribune*, 26 March, 1965.

13 Church, Ruth Ellen. "Women Learn Wine Makes Table Pretty." *Chicago Tribune*, 2 Sept. 1966.

14 Olken, Charles. "Thursday Thorns: A Sneak Peak At The SF Chronicle's New Wine Writer." *Connoisseurs' Guide to California Wine*, 6 Aug. 2015, http://www.cgcw.com/databaseshowitem.aspx?id=80704.

15 McInerney, Jay. *The Juice: Vinous Veritas*, First Vintage Books, 2013, pp. 92.

16 Ibid., 128.

17 Mintz, Sidney W. *Sweetness and Power*. Viking, New York, New York, 1985, p. 95.

18 Samenow, Jason, and Kasha Patel. "Record-Setting Cold Snap Hits Europe, Stunning Spring Crops." *Washington Post*, 4 Apr. 2022, https://www.washingtonpost.com/weather/2022/04/04/europe-record-cold-france-agriculture/

19 Camus, Thibault. "Late Frost Ices over French Vineyards, Threatens Fruit Crops." *AP NEWS*, 4 Apr. 2022, https://apnews.com/article/business-france-europe-environment-48f01edff0e6cbc33e4a1b51d36790dc.

20 Kothia, Khadija. "French Wine Production to Plunge as Much as 30% This Year." *Bloomberg*, 6 Aug. 2021, https://www.bloomberg.com/news/articles/2021-08-06/french-wine-production-to-plunge-as-much-as-30-this-year.

21 Michalopoulos, Sarantis. "One French Farmer Commits Suicide Every Two Days, Survey Says." *EURACTIV*, 16 Oct. 2018, https://www.euractiv.com/section/agriculture-food/news/one-french-farmer-commits-suicide-every-two-days-survey-says/.

22 According to Matthew Clarke, Associate Professor of Grape Breeding and Enology at the University of Minnesota.

Chapter 3

1 Porter, Ebenezer. "The Fatal Effects of Ardent Spirits." Florida Atlantic University Digital Library. Peter B. Gleason and Co., printers, Hartford, CT, 1811.

2 Wesley, John. "A Word to a Drunkard." *The Works of the Rev. John Wesley, Volume 8*, J. & J. Harper, New York, 1827, pp. 143–145.

3 Church, Ruth Ellen. "Women Learn Wine Makes Table Pretty." *Chicago Tribune*, 2 Sept. 1966.

4 Elliot, Alistair, and Ovid. "Table Manners for Girls." *Roman Food Poems: A Modern Translation*, Prospect, 2003, p. 17.

5 "Where does the word 'sommelier' come from?" *Wine Spectator.* 1 Dec. 2010. https://www.winespectator.com/articles/where-does-the-word-sommelier-come-from-44160

6 Wise, Jason, director. *Somm*. Forgotten Man Films, 2012.

7 "About/FAQs." *The Court of Master Sommeliers*, https://www.mastersommeliers.org/about.

8 Moskin, Julia. "The Wine World's Most Elite Circle Has a Sexual Harassment Problem." *New York Times*, 29 Oct. 2020, https://www.nytimes.com/2020/10/29/dining/drinks/court-of-master-sommeliers-sexual-harassment-wine.html.

9 Moskin, Julia. "Chairman of Elite Wine Group Resigns Amid Its Sexual Harassment Scandal." *New York Times*, 6 Nov. 2020, https://www.nytimes.com/2020/11/06/dining/drinks/court-master-sommeliers-chairman-resigns.html.

10 Morales, Christina. "Elite Wine Group Moves to Expel 6 Members in Sexual Harassment Inquiry." *New York Times*,

19 Nov. 2021, https://www.nytimes.com/2021/11/19/dining/master-sommeliers-terminated-sexual-harassment.html.

11 *CMS-A Code Ethics and Professional Responsibility*. May 2021, https://www.mastersommeliers.org/sites/default/files/CMS-A%20Code%20Ethics%20and%20Professional%20Responsibility%20%28May%202021%29_0.pdf.

12 Wines, Emily, et al. "Open Letter from the Court of Master Sommeliers, Americas to Survivors of Sexual Misconduct, Harassment or Abuse." Undated.

13 Moskin, Julia. "Chairman of Elite Wine Group Resigns Amid Its Sexual Harassment Scandal." *New York Times*, 6 Nov. 2020, https://www.nytimes.com/2020/11/06/dining/drinks/court-master-sommeliers-chairman-resigns.html.

Chapter 4

1 United States Department of Agriculture: National Agricultural Statistics Service, 2021, *Land Values 2021 Summary*, https://www.nass.usda.gov/Publications/Todays_Reports/reports/land0821.pdf.

2 The vineyard statistic is according to wine country broker David Ashcraft, citing Trends in Ag. Land & Lease Values, ASFMRA-California in 2019.

3 "Heat Illness Prevention in Outdoor Places of Employment." California Code of Regulations, Title 8, Section 3395. Heat Illness Prevention in Outdoor Places of Employment., https://www.dir.ca.gov/title8/3395.html.

4 Brown, Alleen. "Grape Pickers Crash Lavish Sonoma Winery Banquet Demanding Better Wildfire Protections." *The Intercept*, 21 Dec. 2021, https://theintercept.com/2021/12/21/wildfires-wine-country-vineyard-workers/.

5 "Workers United: The Delano Grape Strike and Boycott (U.S. National Park Service)." *National Parks Service*, U.S. Department of the Interior, https://www.nps.gov/articles/000/workers-united-the-delano-grape-strike-and-boycott.htm.

6 Navarro, Juan. "Tres Detenidos En Valladolid Por Esclavizar a Migrantes En La Vendimia." *El Pais*, 4 Oct. 2021, https://elpais.com/espana/2021-10-04/tres-detenidos-en-valladolid-por-esclavizar-a-migrantes-en-la-vendimia.

7 Gautronneau, Vincent. "Les Vendangeurs De Champagne Étaient Traités Comme Des Esclaves." *Le Parisien*, 26 June 2019, https://www.leparisien.fr/faits-divers/les-vendangeurs-de-champagne-etaient-traites-comme-des-esclaves-26-06-2019-8103519.php.

8 According to the California Department of Forestry and Fire Protection (Cal Fire) in a report published January 2022. https://www.fire.ca.gov/media/4jandlhh/top20_acres.pdf

9 Klearman, Sarah. "Preliminary Grape Crush Report Reveals Napa Valley Production down Almost 40%." *Napa Valley Register*, 10 Feb. 2021, https://napavalleyregister.com/news/local/preliminary-grape-crush-report-reveals-napa-valley-production-down-almost-40/article_6af781ed-1fe8-53f5-ba12-16d06a45acf0.html

10 Murray, Maegan. "Grape Vines Exposed to Smoke to Test Taint from Wildfires." *WSU TriCities*, 16 Aug. 2016, https://tricities.wsu.edu/grape-vines-exposed-to-smoke-to-test-taint-from-wildfires/#:~:text=Smoke%20taint%20is%20created%20by,the%20smoky%20aromas%20become%20apparent.%E2%80%9D.

11 According to the US Drought Monitor data tables, specific to California, https://droughtmonitor.unl.edu/DmData/DataTables.aspx?state,ca.

12 Wick, Julia. "As Drought Worsens, Regulators Impose Unprecedented Water Restrictions on California Farms." *Los Angeles Times*, 3 Aug. 2021, https://www.latimes.com /california/story/2021-08-03/water-regulators-impose -restrictions-on-california-farmers.

13 Hamilton, Matt. "Amid Worsening Drought, Lake Oroville's Record-Low Water Level Forces Shutdown of Hydroelectric Power Plant." *Los Angeles Times*, 5 Aug. 2021, https://www .latimes.com/california/story/2021-08-05/amid-worsening -drought-lake-orovilles-record-low-water-level-forces -shutdown-of-hydroelectric-power-plant.

14 Guzman, Joseph. *The Hill*, 17 June 2021, https://thehill.com /changing-america/sustainability/environment/559064 -hundreds-of-thousands-of-salmon-dying-in-climate/.

15 Drawn from https://www.drought.gov/states/california

16 "Hailstorm devastates hundreds of hectares of Bordeaux vines in SW France." *Reuters*. 21 April 2020. https://www .reuters.com/article/us-france-wine/hailstorm-devastates -hundreds-of-hectares-of-bordeaux-vines-in-sw-france -idUSKCN2232NQ

17 Castrolade, Jelisa. "Germany's Wine Country Damaged By Severe Floods." *Food & Wine*, 21 July 2021, https://www .foodandwine.com/news/germany-wine-country-floods.

WORKS CONSULTED

Alice Feiring, *The Battle for Wine and Love: Or How I Saved the World from Parkerization*

Alice Feiring, *To Fall in Love, Drink This*

Ann B. Matasar, *Women of Wine: The Rise of Women in the Global Wine Industry*

Bitter Grapes, documentary directed by Tom Heinemann

Colm Tóibín, *Homage to Barcelona*

Deirdre Heekin, *An Unlikely Vineyard*

Diane Ackerman, *A Natural History of the Senses*

Domestique Wine newsletter

Elin McCoy, *The Emperor of Wine: The Remarkable Story of the Rise and Reign of Robert Parker*

Isabelle Legeron, *Natural Wine: An Introduction to Organic and Biodynamic Wines Made Naturally*

Jason Wilson, *Godforsaken Grapes*

Jay McInerney, *The Juice: Vinous Veritas*

Jonathan Nossiter, *Liquid Memory*

Jorge Martínez Reverte, *La Batalla del Ebro*

Mondovino, documentary directed by Jonathan Nossiter

Nicolas Joly, *Wine from Sky to Earth: Growing & Appreciating Biodynamic Wine*

Pablo Neruda, "Ode to Wine" (poem)

Paul Lukacs, *Inventing Wine*

Pipette Magazine, published by Rachel Signer

Pliny the Elder, *Natural History*

Rachel Signer, *You Had Me at Pét Nat*

Rebel Rebel wine newsletter

Robert White, *Understanding Vineyard Soils*

Robin Wall Kimmerer, *Braiding Sweetgrass: Indigenous Wisdom, Scientific Knowledge, and the Teachings of Plants*

Rod Phillips, *Wine: A Social and Cultural History of the Drink that Changed Our Lives*

Sidney Mintz, *Sweetness and Power: The Place of Sugar in Modern History*

Somm, documentary directed by Jason Wise

The Feiring Line newsletter, published by Alice Feiring

The Wine Zine, published by Katherine Clary

Thomas Pinney, *A History of Wine in America*

Victoria James, *Wine Girl: A Sommelier's Tale of Making It in the Toxic World of Fine Dining*

GLOSSARY

An incomplete, but hopefully helpful, glossary of some wine terms found in the book.

Albariño: A white grape variety, primarily grown on the coast of western Spain and in Portugal. Generally acidic.

Alcoholic fermentation: The chemical process by which yeast consumes grapes' sugar and converts the sugar to alcohol. Carbon dioxide is one byproduct.

Alsace: A region in eastern France at the border with Germany, known for wines made with Gewurztraminer and Riesling grapes.

Alsace Cremant: Sparkling wines from Alsace.

American Viticultural Areas (AVAs): Designated grape-growing regions in the United States (for example, Napa Valley or Paso Robles), indicated on wine labels. To use certain AVAs on labels, winemakers must ensure that at least 85 percent of a wine's volume comes from grapes grown within that region.

American rootstock/Pie americano: A root from the Americas, on which European winemakers often graft their grapes, which is resistant to phylloxera, the blight that decimated Europe's vineyards in the nineteenth century

Appellation d'origine contrôlée (AOC): Similar to AVAs, the French wine zoning system designed to prevent fraud and to indicate wine from certain places as unique. For example, Banyuls (in southwestern France), and Beaujolais.

Barrel/barrica: A vessel usually made of wood in which winemakers leave their wine for years (see aging, or crianza). The barrel imparts certain flavors to the wine. Typical tasting notes include vanilla, tobacco, and clove. Generally, though not always, used for aging red wine. Also used in oxidative and reductive wines.

Beaujolais: French AOC in the Burgundy region; generally known for lighter red wines made from the Gamay grape variety.

Biodynamics: A style of holistic agriculture developed by Rudolf Steiner, a nineteenth-century Austrian philosopher. Central to biodynamics is the notion that an entire farm is a single organism. The goal of biodynamic farmers is to maintain equilibrium between plants, animals, humans, and the soil by nurturing biodiversity through cover crops, usually wild plants that help maintain soil health, and polyculture, the introduction of other plants and herbs into the vineyard.

Blind tasting: Tasting a wine with no knowledge of its identity, often to improve one's palate. Grapes, region, producer, and vintage are unknown to the taster.

Bordeaux: Port city and wine region in western France known for intense red wines made from Merlot and Cabernet Sauvignon grapes.

Botellón: Spanish drinking ritual in which people gather on street corners and plazas to consume.

Brut: French word referring to dry sparkling wines (as opposed to sweeter sparkling wines).

Bud break: A pivotal event in viticulture, harkening the emergence of green shoots from which leaves, stems, and grapes will eventually grow. Springtime in the Northern Hemisphere.

Buds: Growing points on a grapevine that indicate where a leaf grew in the prior season, which represent possible growing points for the upcoming season.

Bulk wine (Vino a granel): Wine shipped in large containers such as tanks or plastic bladders as opposed to bottles or smaller containers.

Cabernet Franc: Red grape variety thought to originate from southwest France. Tasting notes can include vegetal.

Cabernet Sauvignon: Red grape variety grown around the world, but generally associated with Bordeaux, France. High in tannin content; intense, alcoholic wines.

Fermentation cap: A floating "cap" atop fermenting wine created by solid parts of a grape (including stems, seeds, and skins) which have risen to the top due to carbon dioxide. To break up the cap, winemakers perform pumpovers and punchdowns.

Carbonic maceration: A winemaking technique in which winemakers add intact grape bunches to a sealed tank full of carbon dioxide, spurring fermentation within the individual grapes, as opposed to crushing them to spur fermentation. Generally used for light, fresh, non-aged red wines.

Cariñena: Red grape variety (with a separate, white mutation) likely native to northeastern Spain. High in tannins. Used in many wines from Priorat, in Catalonia.

Castilla La-Mancha: Large wine region in central Spain. Hot, dry temperatures create the intense red wines for which the region is known.

Catalonia: Region in northeastern Spain home to Cava, a sparkling white wine.

Central Valley California: A large agricultural region in central California known for bulk wine.

Champagne: A wine region in France and a sparkling winemaking style. Wine undergoes two fermentations, one in the tank and the second, prompted by an addition of sugar, in a bottle. There are seven permitted grapes to make Champagnes, and the most popular are Pinot Noir (red), Pinot Meunier (red) and Chardonnay (white).

Chardonnay: A white grape variety originating from Burgundy, in France. Chardonnays from the Chablis region of Burgundy, for example, tend to be acidic, while Chardonnays from northern California tend to be aged in oak, producing a richer, buttery wine.

Chinon: A town in France's Loire Valley, a central-west region, known for both tart and heavy red wines.

Clarification: A process by which winemakers make a wine more transparent, generally by using additives such as gelatin finings, which remove elements that make a wine cloudy. Generally not done in natural wines. (See also: filtration.)

Co-ferment: To ferment multiple grape varieties simultaneously, or grapes with another fruit, such as pears or apples.

Cordon: A horizontal extension of a grapevine's truck that usually looks like shrugging shoulders.

Cortese: A white grape considered native of Piemonte, Italy, known to be crisp and acidic.

Court of Master Sommeliers: Founded in England in 1977 as an international examining body, the Court offers prestigious certifications to sommeliers who pass its tests. In 2020, the *New York Times* published a report revealing a culture of sexual harassment and assault within the Court.

Cru: French word for growth, which refers to a particular growing site or vineyard. In Burgundy, for example, Grand Crus are considered the best vineyard sites and supposedly yield the highest quality wine.

Cuvée: There are several uses for this word. In sparkling wine, cuvée refers to the first-pressed juice. In still wine, cuvée generally refers to a particular blend of wine, with more than one grape variety.

Denominación de Origen: Designated grape-growing regions in Spain and parts of Latin America.

Diurnal shift: The difference between the nighttime low temperature and the daytime high temperatures, which allows grape ripening to slow and the pH to remain balanced, resulting in a wine that tastes even rather than overly alcoholic or acidic.

Élevage: The wine maturing process/progress between fermentation and bottling. Includes a collection of decisions from a winemaker: What vessel (barrel or tank) should hold the wine; how long the wine should remain on its skins or lees (dead yeast); whether to stop or shorten the malolactic fermentation; and so on. Also called la crianza in Spanish, or aging.

Filtration: A process by which a winemaker pumps wine through cellulose pads or synthetic membranes to clarify and remove unwanted particles

Frontenac: A cold-hardy red grape variety created by the University of Minnesota's grape breeding program, hybridized from Landot Noir and Vitis riparia, an indigenous American grape.

Galicia: A rainy, lush region in northwestern Spain known for its wines made of Albariño grapes.

Gamay: A light red grape variety generally associated with the Beaujolais region.

Garnacha: A late-ripening red grape variety from Spain, decently tannic. Clones include white and gray varieties.

Graciano: A red grape variety from Spain, acidic and moderately tannic.

Graft/injertar: To insert a shoot (such as a vine shoot) into a trunk or stem so they grow together. In vineyards, winemakers often graft specific grape varieties to American rootstock.

Hundred Point Scale: A way to rank wines based on Robert Parker's popular system in the *Wine Advocate* that assigns wines scores based on color and appearance; aroma; flavor; and overall quality.

Jory soil: A volcanic soil in Oregon's Willamette Valley derived from igneous Columbia River basalt. Pinot Noir wines grown in this soil tend to be lighter in color and taste of red berries, such as raspberries and cherries.

The Jura: A small region in eastern France along the Swiss border, increasingly known for natural wines (and devastated by climate change).

L'Albera: A Catalan mountain range, the easternmost extension of the Pyrenees; what I came to consider a wine region unto itself.

La Crescent: A cold-hardy white grape developed by the University's of Minnesota's grape breeding program. Its ancestry is complex, including a variety of Muscat from the Vitis vinifera side, and indigenous vines like Labrusca and Riparia.

Llicorella: Soil made of quartz slate with layers of clay, found in Catalonia.

Maceration: The process of leaving fermenting grape juice (and the post-fermentation wine) in contact with skins, stems, and seeds. Extended maceration can last days, weeks, or months.

Malolactic fermentation: After alcoholic fermentation, a secondary process in which bacteria convert tart malic acid into softer lactic acid, making red wines (and some whites) smoother and creamier rather than sharp and acidic.

Malvasia de Sitges: An aromatic white grape found in the Mediterranean, especially around Catalonia's towns of Sitges and Garraf.

Marquette: A cold-hardy red grape variety developed by the University of Minnesota's grape breeding program, hybridized from other complex hybrids. A cousin of Frontenac.

Master of Wine: A prestigious title for wine industry professionals who have passed an exam testing their tasting skills; theoretical knowledge; and understanding of the science and business of wine.

Merlot: An intense, spicy red grape variety associated with Bordeaux and Apalta in north-central Chile.

Microbiota: All the microorganisms in a particular site; in the case of this book, soil.

Minerality: What wine writer Jancis Robinson calls an "an elusive wine characteristic," minerality is a descriptor of a wine's tastes/smells/textures similar to chalk, flint, and wet stone.

Napa Valley: An AVA in northern California especially well known for Cabernet Sauvignon. Central to America's high-end wine industry.

Native yeast/levadura autóctona: Yeasts occurring naturally on grape skins and in the environment, as opposed to cultured yeasts, which are specifically manufactured for winemaking. (See also: spontaneous fermentation.)

Natural wine: More of a philosophy than a stable definition, such wines, which have no regulatory body determining what is and is not "natural," are generally made from grapes grown without pesticides, and have no chemical additions during the winemaking process itself—except, perhaps, a small amount of sulfites to keep the wine stable for overseas shipment.

Orange wine: Wine made from white grapes with their skins left on, creating an orange-like hue.

Oxidative wine: Wines that are intentionally exposed to oxygen (for example, Sherry), often by letting a wine age in a partially-filled barrel. Spain's rancios are oxidative wines.

Panal: A sandy soil formed by the fossils of sea creatures, found in the Catalan region of Terra Alta.

Piemonte: A region in northwest Italy bordering France and Switzerland known for Barolo, strong wines made from Nebbiolo grapes.

Pigéage/Foot tread/Punchdown: A process during fermentation by which winemakers stomp on the wine's cap or push the material back down to the bottom with a tool that looks like a massive potato masher to avoid bacterial buildup and extract tannins, color, and aromas/flavors from the wine's solid elements.

Pinot Gris (Pinot Grigio): A white grape variety mutated from Pinot Noir, with high acidity. American Pinot Gris often have more fruit flavors.

Pinot Noir: A light red grape variety likely from Burgundy, France, but planted around the world, and especially well-known in Oregon.

Porrón: A glass wine pitcher from Catalonia, great for parties.

Powdery mildew: A fungal disease that often infects grapevines during periods of humidity, identifiable for white powdery spots on the leaf.

Press (grapes): To extract juice from grapes. White grapes tend to (though not always) be pressed immediately after harvesting. There are several ways to press grapes, including foot treading, basket pressing (small, more traditional barrel-shaped presses with slats to allow juice to run out), and membrane/bladder pressing (which expand with air or water to crush grapes at a larger scale), among others.

Priorat: A high-end wine region in Catalonia known for terraced vineyards and llicorella soil, and home of the monastery Escaladei.

Prosecco: A white grape (also called Glera) that is primarily used in sparkling Italian wine of the same name.

Pruning: Cutting back vine branches to remove excess buds and encourage vigorous, limited grape growth on vines. In the Northern Hemisphere, farmers prune in the winter.

Pumpover: A cellar process by which winemakers pump grape juice from the bottom to the top of a tank and splash it over the cap to mix the solids back in with the liquids to release flavor, color, and aroma from the solids.

Racking/trasiego: A cellar process done after fermentation by which winemakers siphon wine between tanks to separate liquid from sediment. Usually repeated several times before bottling.

Ramification: When grapevine roots branch off to absorb minerals, making healthier and higher quality grapes. Often done in nutrient-poor soil conditions.

Red wine: Wine made primarily from red grape varieties, often higher in alcohol content and tannins than white wine.

Reductive wine: Wine intentionally made with limited oxygen contact, even less than is normal in winemaking.

Refractometer: A telescope-like instrument used measure sugar levels in grapes; generally helps to determine when a vineyard is ready for harvesting.

Residual sugar: Natural sugars leftover in wine after the fermentation process is complete.

Riesling: A light colored and aromatic white grape variety native to Germany.

Rosé: A style of wine with red grapes made by removing grape skins, stems, and seeds quickly after pressing to give the wine a pinkish hue and less tannic structure than a longer macerated red wine.

Sauló: Sandy granite soil, found in Catalonia.

Sauv Blanc (Sauvignon blanc): A French white grape variety now widely planted around the world; generally light in color.

Savennières: A white wine AOC in France's Loire Valley, known for wines made from acidic Chenin blanc grapes.

Shear: Thick, scissors-like tools used to chop through grapevines during pruning.

Shiraz (Australian usage)/Syrah: A red grape variety that tends to produce intense and dark-fruit flavored wines.

Shoots: The primary unit of growth in a grapevine, made up of leaves and stems.

Smoke taint: A broad term for what happens when grapes are exposed to wildfire smoke. Smoke molecules bind with sugar, the compound that makes fermentation possible, making smoke taint nearly impossible to extract. Can change the taste and smell of a wine.

Sobremesa: In Spain, the period of time after the official meal, in which guests talk and pick at dessert, drink rancios or liquor, drink espresso and coffee, etc. Lingering. Can last for hours.

Sommelier: A person who serves wine. Depending on the setting and the level of official certification, the job takes on many more meanings. Sommeliers have in-depth knowledge about wines—where they come from, how they taste, how they're made—and guide customers on what to order. They sometimes create wine lists for restaurants.

Sonoma: A wine region in northern California, neighboring Napa Valley. Closer to the coast, it's known for large diurnal shifts—hot days and cool nights, thanks to fog from the ocean.

Spontaneous fermentation/ Fermentación espontánea: The fermentation that occurs when a winemaker does not interfere with the yeast and bacteria in contact with grape juice. In other words, naturally occurring fermentation with whatever yeasts and bacteria already exist on the grape skins and in the cellar environment. Championed by natural winemakers.

Sulfites: A chemical compound (sulfur dioxide) that naturally occurs in low levels during winemaking. Sulfites are also added to wines at various stages of the process—during fermentation, just before bottling—to help make the wine more shelf stable. Natural winemakers generally do not add sulfites (those who don't add them often call their wines 0/0).

Sumoll: A rare red grape variety native to Catalonia.

Systematic Approach to Tasting: Created by the Wine and Spirit Education Trust (WSET), a tasting guide which offers a protocol and a set of terms for how drinkers should taste wine, starting with an examination of the wine's appearance and ending with its flavors.

Tannins: Compounds found in grape skins, stems, and seeds that give a wine its astringency. Red wines tend to be more tannic because they are aged with skins for longer periods of time than white wines.

Tempranillo: An early-ripening red grape variety from Spain associated with the Rioja region, which produces intense, tannic, but also acidic wines.

Terra Alta: A mountainous region in southern Catalonia thought to have inspired Pablo Picasso's cubism. Known for wines made of Vernatxa grapes (local dialect for Garnacha). Four hours south and inland of L'Albera.

Tramuntana: Catalan for "across the mountains," a wind that blows south from France over the Pyrenees at random intervals throughout the year, usually in the spring and winter.

Trellised vine/viña espaldera: Vines that are grown vertically with the support of a wire. (As opposed to en vaso, or goblet training, in which vines grow without wire support, as if a bush.)

Variety (grape): The type of grape.

Vendimia: The grape harvest in Spanish-speaking countries

Veraison: The onset of ripening when the vines transition from energy production, photosynthesis, to energy consumption, which gives size and color to the grapes.

Verdejo: A light white grape, primarily grown in Castilla-León, Spain.

Vineyard orientation: The axis on which a vineyard is planted, i.e. north-south or east-west. It's generally seen as preferable to plant north-south for more uniform sun exposure, though a region's particular geography also affects sun exposure.

Vintage/Añada: The year a wine's grapes were harvested. A wine made from grapes picked in 2013, for example, would be considered a 2013 vintage.

Volatility: Otherwise known as Volatile Acidity, or VA; a measure of a wine's gaseous acids. Winemakers are often concerned with acetic acid, which smells and tastes of vinegar, and ethyl acetate, which smells and tastes of nail polish remover.

White wine: Wine made primarily from white grape varieties. Usually, though not always, the grape skins are removed shortly after pressing.

Willakenzie soil: Found in Oregon's Willamette Valley; a soil formed from loose loamy sandstone that drains well, and, with Pinot Noir, tends to produce dark, strong wines that taste of blackberries and plums.

Willamette Valley: A fertile agricultural and viticultural region by Oregon's Coast Range to the west and Cascade Range to the east. Its three main soils are volcanic, sedimentary, and silty, and the region is known for wines made from Pinot Noir.

Wine aroma wheel: Created by University of California, Davis chemist Ann C. Noble in the 1980s; a circle containing dozens of possible aromas to be found in wine. With the wheel, Noble attempted to make wine more accessible to everyday drinkers by creating a common language.

Wine future: Young wines purchased before they've been bottled, the final quality unknown.

WORKS CITED

"About/FAQs." *The Court of Master Sommeliers*, https://www
    .mastersommeliers.org/about#:~:text=There%20are%20172
    %20professionals%20who,first%20Master%20Sommelier%20
    Diploma%20Exam.

Agencia Estatal de Meteorologia. "El Año 2017 Fue El Más Cálido
    y El Segundo Más Seco En España Desde 1965 ." *AEMET,
    Spain*, 10 Jan. 2018, http://www.aemet.es/en/noticias/2018/01/
    Resumen_climatico_2017.

"Appellation D'origine Controlée (AOC)." *Champagne.fr*, https://
    www.champagne.fr/en/terroir-appellation/appellation/
    appellation-origine-controlee-aoc.

Brown, Alleen. "Grape Pickers Crash Lavish Sonoma Winery
    Banquet Demanding Better Wildfire Protections." *The Intercept*,
    21 Dec. 2021, https://theintercept.com/2021/12/21/wildfires
    -wine-country-vineyard-workers/.

Burns, Scott. "The Importance of Soil and Geology in Tasting
    Terroir with a Case History from the Willamette Valley,
    Oregon." *The Geography of Wine*, 2011, pp. 95–108., https://doi
    .org/10.1007/978-94-007-0464-0_6.

Camus, Thibault. "Late Frost Ices over French Vineyards,
    Threatens Fruit Crops." *AP NEWS*, 4 Apr. 2022, https://apnews
    .com/article/business-france-europe-environment-48f01edff0e
    6cbc33e4a1b51d36790dc.

Castrolade, Jelisa. "Germany's Wine Country Damaged By Severe Floods." *Food & Wine*, 21 July 2021, https://www.foodandwine.com/news/germany-wine-country-floods.

Church, Ruth Ellen. "Do Wines Make Women Giggly?" *Chicago Tribune*, 1965.

Church, Ruth Ellen. "Women Learn Wine Making." *Chicago Tribune*, 2 Sept. 1966.

CMS-A Code Ethics and Professional Responsibility (May 2021). May 2021, https://www.mastersommeliers.org/sites/default/files/CMS-A%20Code%20Ethics%20and%20Professional%20Responsibility%20%28May%202021%29_0.pdf.

"Discover Ann Noble's Aroma Wheel." *Discover Ann Noble's Aroma Wheel*, https://www.winearomawheel.com/ann-noble-aroma-wheel.html.

"Domaine De La Romane-Conti." *Conti*, http://m.romanee-conti.fr/familles.php.

Elliot, Alistair, and Ovid. "Table Manners for Girls." *Roman Food Poems: A Modern Translation*, Prospect, Devon, UK, 2003, p. 17.

Evans-Pritchard, E. E. "Nuer Time-Reckoning." *Africa*, vol. 12, no. 2, 1939, pp. 189–216., https://doi.org/10.2307/1155085.

Farmer, Erica A. "Codifying Consensus and Constructing Boundaries: Setting the Limits of *Appellation D'origine Contrôlée* Protection in Bordeaux, France." *PoLAR: Political and Legal Anthropology Review*, vol. 37, no. 1, 2014, pp. 126–144., https://doi.org/10.1111/plar.12054.

Gautronneau, Vincent. "Les Vendangeurs De Champagne Étaient Traités Comme Des Esclaves." *Le Parisien*, 26 June 2019, https://www.leparisien.fr/faits-divers/les-vendangeurs-de-champagne-etaient-traites-comme-des-esclaves-26-06-2019-8103519.php.

"Grand Cru Classes EN 1855." *Site Officiel Bordeaux.com*, https://www.bordeaux.com/gb/Our-Terroir/Classifications/Grand-Cru-Classes-en-1855.

Guzman, Joseph. "Hundreds of thousands of salmon dying in 'climate catastrophe.'" *The Hill*, 17 June 2021, https://thehill .com/changing-america/sustainability/environment/559064 -hundreds-of-thousands-of-salmon-dying-in-climate/.

Hamilton, Matt. "Amid Worsening Drought, Lake Oroville's Record-Low Water Level Forces Shutdown of Hydroelectric Power Plant." *Los Angeles Times*, 5 Aug. 2021, https://www .latimes.com/california/story/2021-08-05/amid-worsening -drought-lake-orovilles-record-low-water-level-forces -shutdown-of-hydroelectric-power-plant.

Jordans, Frank. "Costly Frost in France Attributed to Climate Change." *AP NEWS*, 15 June 2021, https://apnews.com/article /france-europe-science-climate-climate-change-73aef640aae ee774cdfbe9159cdc87c9.

Klearman, Sarah. "Preliminary Grape Crush Report Reveals Napa Valley Production down Almost 40%." *Napa Valley Register*, 10 Feb. 2021, https://napavalleyregister.com/news /local/preliminary-grape-crush-report-reveals-napa-valley -production-down-almost-40/article_6af781ed-1fe8-53f5-ba12 -16d06a45acf0.html#:~:text=Napa%20County%27s%20wine %20industry%20crushed,40%25%20decline%20year%20over %20year.

Kothia, Khadija. "French Wine Production to Plunge as Much as 30% This Year." *Bloomberg*, 6 Aug. 2021, https://www .bloomberg.com/news/articles/2021-08-06/french-wine -production-to-plunge-as-much-as-30-this-year.

Leitao, David D. "The Thigh Birth of Dionysus: Exploring Legitimacy in the Classical City-State." *The Pregnant Male as Myth and Metaphor in Classical Greek Literature*, Cambridge University Pres, New York City, 2014, pp. 58–99.

Leon, Miguel de. "It's Time to Decolonize Wine." *PUNCH*, 26 June 2020, https://punchdrink.com/articles/time-to-decolonize -wine-sommelier-racism-restaurants/.

Matasar, Ann B. "Women Need Not Apply." *Women of Wine: The Rise of Women in the Global Wine Industry*, University of California Press, Berkeley, 2010, p. 10.

McCoy, Elin. *The Emperor of Wine: The Remarkable Story of the Rise and Reign of Robert Parker*, Grub Street, London, 2008, p. 98.

McInerney, Jay. *The Juice: Vinous Veritas*, First Vintage Books, New York, NY, 2013, pp. 92, 128.

Mejia, Paula. "The Gnarled History of Los Angeles's Vineyards." *Atlas Obscura*, Atlas Obscura, 3 July 2018, https://www.atlasobscura.com/articles/history-of-california-wine.

Michalopoulos, Sarantis. "One French Farmer Commits Suicide Every Two Days, Survey Says." *Www.euractiv.com*, EURACTIV, 16 Oct. 2018, https://www.euractiv.com/section/agriculture-food/news/one-french-farmer-commits-suicide-every-two-days-survey-says/.

Mintz, Sidney W. *Sweetness and Power*. Viking, 1985.

Mobley, Esther. "Wine's Diversity Issue Starts with the Way We Talk about the Taste of Wine." *San Francisco Chronicle*, 8 Sept. 2020, https://www.sfchronicle.com/wine/article/Wine-s-diversity-issue-starts-with-the-way-we-15544232.php.

Morales, Christina. "Elite Wine Group Moves to Expel 6 Members in Sexual Harassment Inquiry." *New York Times*, 19 Nov. 2021, https://www.nytimes.com/2021/11/19/dining/master-sommeliers-terminated-sexual-harassment.html.

Moskin, Julia. "Chairman of Elite Wine Group Resigns Amid Its Sexual Harassment Scandal." *New York Times*, 6 Nov. 2020, https://www.nytimes.com/2020/11/06/dining/drinks/court-master-sommeliers-chairman-resigns.html.

Moskin, Julia. "The Wine World's Most Elite Circle Has a Sexual Harassment Problem." *New York Times*, 29 Oct. 2020, https://www.nytimes.com/2020/10/29/dining/drinks/court-of-master-sommeliers-sexual-harassment-wine.html.

Murray, Maegan. "Grape Vines Exposed to Smoke to Test Taint
    from Wildfires." *WSU TriCities*, 16 Aug. 2016, https://tricities
    .wsu.edu/grape-vines-exposed-to-smoke-to-test-taint-from
    -wildfires/#:~:text=Smoke%20taint%20is%20created%20by,the
    %20smoky%20aromas%20become%20apparent.%E2%80%9D.

Navarro, Juan. "Tres Detenidos En Valladolid Por Esclavizar a
    Migrantes En La Vendimia." *El Pais*, 4 Oct. 2021, https://www
    .google.com/url?q=https://elpais.com/espana/2021-10-04/tres
    -detenidos-en-valladolid-por-esclavizar-a-migrantes-en-la
    -vendimia.html&sa=D&source=docs&ust=1663791064450853
    &usg=AOvVaw252FyvBYa2zCzug9BkvqXf.

Olken, Charles. "Thursday Thorns: A Sneak Peak At The
    SF Chronicle's New Wine Writer." *Connoisseurs' Guide
    to California Wine*, 6 Aug. 2015, http://www.cgcw.com/
    databaseshowitem.aspx?id=80704.

O'Keefe, Kerin. "The Volcanic Wines of Italy." *Wine Enthusiast*,
    16 Jan. 2018, https://www.winemag.com/2018/01/16/volcanic
    -wines-italy/.

Pinney, Thomas. "Chapter 8, Eastern Viticulture Comes of Age:
    The Grape Boom in the Old South." *A History of Wine in
    America*, UC Press E-Books Collection, 1982–2004, 1989,
    https://publishing.cdlib.org/ucpressebooks/view?docId
    =ft967nb63q&chunk.id=d0e6202&toc.id=d0e5748&toc.depth
    =1&brand=ucpress&anchor.id=bkd0e6311#X.

"Pliny the Elder, the Natural History John Bostock, M.D., F.R.S.,
    H.T. Riley, Esq., B.A., Ed." *Pliny the Elder, The Natural History,
    BOOK I.1, DEDICATION. 1 Lemaire Informs Us, in His Title-
    Page, That the Two First Books of the Natural History Are Edited
    by M. Alexandre, in His Edition.*, https://www.perseus.tufts.edu/
    hopper/text?doc=Plin.%2BNat.%2Btoc.

"Pliny the Elder, the Natural History John Bostock, M.D.,
    F.R.S., H.T. Riley, Esq., B.A., Ed." *Pliny the Elder, The Natural
    History, BOOK XVII. THE NATURAL HISTORY OF THE*

*CULTIVATED TREES., CHAP. 3.-WHAT SOILS ARE TO BE
CONSIDERED THE BEST.*, http://www.perseus.tufts.edu/
hopper/text?doc=Perseus%3Atext%3A1999.02.0137%3Abook
%3D17%3Achapter%3D3.

Pomranz, Mike. "This Is the World's Most Expensive Bottle of
Wine." *Food & Wine*, Food & Wine, 16 Oct. 2018, https://
www.foodandwine.com/news/most-expensive-wine-auction
-romanee-conti-burgundy.

Reverte, Jorge Martiínez. *La Batalla Del Ebro*. Planeta DeAgostini,
2005.

Richard Woodard, "DRC 1945 Sets Record for Wine Auction
Price." *Decanter*, 16 Oct. 2018, https://www.decanter.com/wine
-news/1945-drc-wine-auction-record-403025/.

Robinson, Jancis. "Castilla-La Mancha." *Castilla-La Mancha |
JancisRobinson.com*, https://www.jancisrobinson.com/learn/
wine-regions/spain/castilla-la-mancha#:~:text=La%20Mancha
%20itself%20is%20Europe%27s,such%20as%20brandy%20de
%20Jerez.

Samenow , Jason, and Kasha Patel. "Record-Setting Cold Snap Hits
Europe, Stunning Spring Crops." *The Washington Post*, 2022.

Smith, Christian. "Five of the Most Expensive Bottles of Wine in
the World." *The Drinks Business*, 10 Mar. 2022, https://www
.thedrinksbusiness.com/2022/03/five-of-the-most-expensive
-bottles-of-wine-in-the-world/.

The Soils | Do Empordà. https://www.doemporda.cat/en/the-soils
.html.

staff, Science X. "Why Odors Trigger Powerful Memories." *Medical
Xpress - Medical Research Advances and Health News*, Medical
Xpress, 8 Mar. 2021, https://medicalxpress.com/news/2021-03
-odors-trigger-powerful-memories.html.

Trenda, Eloise. "Wine Production Volume in Spain by Region."
Statista, 8 Feb. 2022, https://www.statista.com/statistics/463936
/production-volume-of-wine-in-spain-by-region/.

United States Department of Agriculture: National Agricultural Statistics Service, 2021, *Land Values 2021 Summary*, https://www.nass.usda.gov/Publications/Todays_Reports/reports/land0821.pdf.

Wesley, John. "A Word to a Drunkard." *The Works of the Rev. John Wesley, Volume 8*, J. & J. Harper, New York, NY, 1827, pp. 143–145.

"What Is Biodynamics?" *What Is Biodynamics? | Biodynamic Association*, https://www.biodynamics.com/what-is-biodynamics.

"What We Do." *WSET*, https://www.wsetglobal.com/about-us/what-we-do/.

White, Robert. *Understanding Vineyard Soils*, Oxford University Press, New York City, 2009, p. 8.

Wick, Julia. "As Drought Worsens, Regulators Impose Unprecedented Water Restrictions on California Farms." *Los Angeles Times*, 3 Aug. 2021, https://www.latimes.com/california/story/2021-08-03/water-regulators-impose-restrictions-on-california-farmers.

Williams, Gavin. "Slaves, Workers, and Wine: The 'Dop System' in the History of the Cape Wine Industry, 1658–1894." *Journal of Southern African Studies*, vol. 42, no. 5, 2016, pp. 893–909., https://doi.org/10.1080/03057070.2016.1234120.

Wilson, Jason. "Dangerous Grapes." *Godforsaken Grapes: A Slightly Tipsy Journey through the World of Strange, Obscure, and Underappreciated Wine*, Abrams Books, 2018, p. 15.

Wise, Jason, director. *Somm*. *Amazon*, 2012, https://www.amazon.com/Somm-Brian-McClintic/dp/B01M27DQH2.

"Workers United: The Delano Grape Strike and Boycott (U.S. National Park Service)." *National Parks Service*, U.S. Department of the Interior, https://www.nps.gov/articles/000/workers-united-the-delano-grape-strike-and-boycott.htm.

"§3395. Heat Illness Prevention in Outdoor Places of Employment." *California Code of Regulations, Title 8, Section 3395. Heat Illness Prevention in Outdoor Places of Employment*, https://www.dir.ca.gov/title8/3395.html.

INDEX